AGE OF THE MASTERS

AGE OF

THE MASTERS

A PERSONAL VIEW OF MODERN ARCHITECTURE

REYNER BANHAM

Icon Editions
Harper & Row, Publishers
New York, Evanston, San Francisco, London

FIRST U.S. EDITION

ISBN: 0-06-430369-1 (cloth) 0-06-430064-1 (paper)

LIBRARY OF CONGRESS CATALOG CARD NUMBER:
74-25276

Designed by Michael Reid

75 76 77 78 79 10 9 8 7 6 5 4 3 2 1

CONTENTS

INTRODUCTION

Ludwig Mies, who later added his mother's name Van der Rohe, was born in Aachen in 1888, worked almost entirely in Berlin until 1937 when he transferred to Chicago for the rest of his life. Although his most famous buildings were probably the German Pavilion in Barcelona in 1929, and the Seagram building in New York (see p 112), his influence can be seen in every square glass office-block in any downtown in the world, and he finally paid handsome tribute to the Berlin tradition in which he grew up with the great museum there (see p 164) completed not long before his death in 1969. Readings: Arthur Drexler, *Mies van der Rohe* (Braziller, Masters of Modern Architecture series), Werner Blaser, *Mies van der Rohe* (Thames & Hudson, 1965).

Ludwig Mies van der Rohe

Walter Gropius

The life of **Frank Lloyd Wright** is becoming the best known of all architectural biographies. Its long span – he lived from 1869 until 1959 and just failed to reach ninety – covered more than half the history of the USA, and embraced sundry periods of his own professional activity. Of these the first notable one ran from 1893, when he set up in independent practice, until 1910 when he left Chicago for Berlin under a cloud. The next did not begin until after 1930 when his fortunes as an architect at last began to revive, and he then enjoyed nearly thirty years of floodlit senescence, of which the first two decades produced some of the best buildings of his whole career, and the last five years some of the silliest projects ever conceived by an old man, anywhere.

Frank Lloyd Wright

Le Corbusier

As one of the generation who grew up with modern architecture – I was born in the year of Le Corbusier's first modern house in Paris – I feel involved for ever with the Masters of the Modern Movement. I had the good luck to meet nearly all of them – Le Corbusier, Frank Lloyd Wright, Walter Gropius, Richard Neutra, Mies van der Rohe – and for me, as for three generations of architects, they were father-figures who commanded awe and suspicion, affection, respect and the normal pains of the generation gap.

Now that they are all dead it is difficult not to feel liberation as well as loss. While they lived they tyrannised the Modern Movement, monopolising attention and preventing the recognition of other (not always lesser) talents. The powerful example of their work seemed to circumscribe the range of action of architects all over the world – it seems as if only a really hard nut like Bruce Goff could seriously attempt any solutions not foreshadowed in their works. But we knew where we stood; they were in charge; they gave security and solidarity to the Movement – and we gave them a kind of loyalty that artists never gave to Picasso, nor musicians to Stravinsky.

The first version of this book was written while they were all still alive – no, Wright and Mendelsohn were already dead but they could still be felt as presences. What I wrote then was intended to introduce readers to a movement in being, a coherent body of works and principles and the men who had invented both. The process of growing out of the International Style – modern architecture's 'Teenage Uniform' as I could already call it – was observably in train, but the principles and precepts that underlay the style looked perfectly secure. Not now – the voices crying in such comfortable wildernesses as university architecture-schools for a return to 'the certainties of the Twenties' and a restoration of the 'Heroic Age of Modern Architecture', are the voices of the lost sons of departed father

figures. The old routines of modern architecture had provided them, and the rest of us, with the emotional and intellectual supports of a familiar language; literally so for the academics; linguistic and semantic studies increasingly provided their models for the understanding of modern architecture. It was a false and doomed understanding; it treated modern architecture as a dead language like Sanskrit, codified its usages and dissected them with high philological professionalism.

Unfortunately the compelling and everchanging demands of man's physical environment won't wait around for academics to 'purify the language of the tribe', to borrow poetry's most famous justification; architecture must move with the times because it helps to create the times. Far more than painting and sculpture and poetry and music, which are only arts, illuminating the nature of our human world, architecture is physically part of that human world. 'You can kill a man with a building as well as an axe', said the German satirist, Heinrich Zille, identifying the mortal dimension by which architecture stands above the mere arts.

That is – in part – why architecture moving with its times will always seem 'difficult' to timid souls who haven't the guts to be more than mere art-lovers, and likewise why it can provoke urban guerillas to desperate action. It is more than a commentary on the human condition – along with war and peace and love and death and pestilence and birth, abundance, disaster and the air we breathe, it *is* the human condition. Modern architecture, in whatever guise and style, represents an ancient craft trying to keep pace with a technological situation that has long since transcended the handicrafts on which architecture was based, in a cultural context that has equally transcended that cosy little Mediterranean basin in which architecture as we know it was first practised as a self-conscious professional skill. If, at the present time, many of us

Walter Gropius's long career in modern architecture – he was born in 1883 and lived until 1969 – was both splendid and baffling, and no historian has yet tried to sum it up. Few men have done more to create the mental and moral climate that made modern architecture possible, none has so consistently hidden his own light under a bushel of collaborators while never escaping public notice for a minute, and none died so execrated for his alleged betrayals – his parts in the design of the PanAm tower over Grand Central Station in New York and the Playboy Club in London will not be forgiven for a generation. Nevertheless, as the founder of the Bauhaus school (1919–1933) he taught the principles of modern design to the world, and the best single reading is still: Walter Gropius, *The New Architecture and the Bauhaus* (Faber)

Le Corbusier, born Charles Edouard Jeanneret in Switzerland in 1888, died famous and French in 1965, All his life he preferred to present himself as a lonely and misunderstood rebel, but – apart from a bad patch in the Thirties – his success and prestige grew steadily until, after the completion of the *Unité* at Marseilles (see p 110) he dominated the world architectural scene as no-one else had done since the time of Michelangelo. Readings: Charles Jencks, *Le Corbusier: the tragic sense in architecture* (Pelican paperback), Francoise Choay, *Le Corbusier* (Braziller, Masters of Modern Architecture series) and for those who have access to specialised libraries, the eight volumes of his *Oeuvre Complète*.

3

**Aldo Loris Rossi and
Donatella Mazzoleni:**
Materiel Habitable, 1970

(including architects) begin to doubt if architecture has the resources to accomplish the tasks which its times demand, and to which the ambitions of the Masters committed it, one should note that architects seem to be almost the only people to notice that some of these tasks even exist, let alone might be accomplished. Their arrogance is appalling, but also encouraging. The demand of the Masters of the Modern Movement that architecture should respond unreservedly to the present time, however deep its roots were struck in past traditions, has forced their followers to accept moral responsibility for virtually the whole of the human environment. To do so involves great sacrifice; the comforts of working within a single coherent style, however 'modern', were comforts that had to be sacrificed sooner or later. They weren't sacrificed, in fact, until the Masters were dead, though weird things had begun to happen in their declining years and even in their own work. Yet the building with

which this book closes, the National Gallery in Berlin, completed not long before its architect, Mies van der Rohe, finally died in 1969, is still couched in The True Style. It closes the book, and an epoch which we can still see as a whole – yet as early as 1960 Philip Johnson, once Mies's truest disciple, was rejoicing that modern architecture had moved into a period of 'murky chaos'. Even so, I doubt if he could have foreseen the shockwaves of doubt that were to convulse the profession before that troubled decade was out.

The gravest of all doubts was whether – or how – architects could continue to sustain their traditional role as form-givers, creators and controllers of human environments. On the one hand were those who condemned the role as elitism; there grew up a kind of environmental populism, a demand for participation by the public, for the right of the people to determine their own environments – all of which was not so

Peter Cook of Archigram:
Plug-In City, 1964

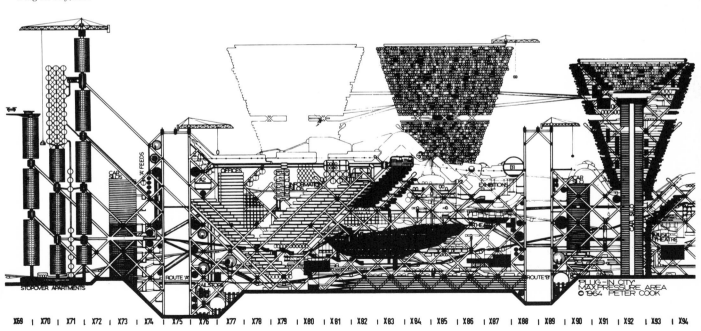

totally unlike the ever-present concept of the modern architect as the humble servant of social need.

On the other hand were those who – not always old or reactionary – maintained that this populism was the road to visual and environmental chaos, a formless world where the people would flounder incomprehending in a mess of their own unwitting creation. Out of such irreconcilable contradictions arose the other characteristic monument of the epoch's ending, the Megastructure. Many were conceived, few were built, but all tended toward a vision of a vast monumental framework of structure, transportation and services, within which individuals or groups or whole communities could contrive their own environments. Such were the 'Plug-In' cities of the English Archigram Group, such also was the project by Aldo Loris Rossi in Naples, who won a major international competition with a project for a half-mile-high slab of 'Habitable Material' from which the inhabitants could sculpt their own whereabouts – these and all the others were in their various ways attempts to reconcile the irreconcilable: the freedom of the individual and the mastery of architecture.

These Megastructures were praised for their daring or damned, according to taste, as monumental follies. They remain a bold, if doomed, attempt by the Modern Movement to save itself by its own efforts and out of its own resources and traditions. It seems at the time of writing that they may not, after all, be architecture's next future, but they represent an heroic attempt to take the future in hand and cast it in an architectural mould. Even when modern architecture seemed plunged in its worst confusions it could still summon up a burst of creative energy that gave the lie to premature reports of its demise. Modern architecture is dead; long live modern architecture!

THEORY

8

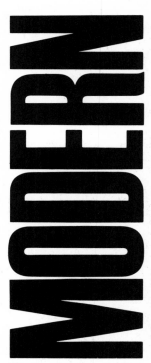

MODERN

Whatever happened to that old modern architecture?
Edward Durell Stone

Charles Rennie
Mackintosh: *Glasgow
School of Art, 1898 onwards*

**Charles Rennie
Mackintosh**, 1868–1928, was
the last British architect of
undoubted genius. His
creative career effectively
spanned the last decade of
the nineteenth century and
the first decade of our own;
his best work was all in and
around the city of Glasgow,
where the citizens have
permitted a few small samples
to remain. Understandably,
he died in exile in England.

What then was this modern architecture that
was dead, yet lived? Its modernity had been
arguable for some years before Ed Stone
formulated his puzzled enquiry. As early as the
Fifties it had become customary to speak of
Modern Architecture as 'mature,' or grown up,
and if that was a meaningful way to talk, then
the word *modern*, in that context, could no
longer have the attributes of bang-up-to-date,
born-yesterday, as-of-now, that it has in
common parlance. All that it could seem to
mean was 'not old,' on the basis of a boundary
between the old and the new that had a fixed
place in time, as between B.C. and A.D. for
example.

For the art of painting, the date that divides the
new from the old is tacitly allowed to be
somewhere in the Impressionist period, around
1870. For architecture it is somewhere around
1900, in the period of the style known as Art
Nouveau. Whether one takes Art Nouveau to be
the last of the old-fashioned styles, or the first of
the new-fangled ones, it can be agreed that this
period represents the division between new and
old, because most of the attributes of the new, or
modern architecture, appeared during the bare
fifteen turbulent years in which the style
flourished, even if no building of the period
quite warrants the label 'modern'.

The School of Art in Glasgow, designed on
both sides of 1900 by Charles Rennie
Mackintosh, is a case in point. In practically
every aspect, the manner of building balances

uneasily between old and new, one thing leaning
a little towards the old, something else
balancing it out by inclining towards the
purely modern. Its materials – masonry, brick,
wood and wrought iron – are not modern, nor is
the continual reliance on handicraft techniques
and applied decoration. Yet the kind of building
Mackintosh made out of these materials and
methods is, in some crucial aspects,
unmistakably modern. In almost every part it is
honest to the point of brutal frankness in its use
of materials; the construction is not disguised:
at the most the brick is painted over, the
woodwork stained, but only walls that will need
a lot of upkeep are plastered and gloss-painted
so that one cannot see whether they are brick or
masonry underneath, and the masonry does not
conceal a steel frame.

About the way the structure works, there is a
similar frankness, but it is made demonstrative:
as with many modernists after him, so with
Mackintosh, structure must not only be done, it
must manifestly be seen to be done. A row of
brick arches, massive as those in a mediaeval
crypt, erupt on the very top floor of the building,
kingposts in roof-trusses are often of
exaggerated dimensions, and when a beam has
to meet a post, rather than spoil beautiful
timbers by notching them and concealing their
mutual support, he twins the beam, and takes
each half of it past the post, which is gripped
between the two halves. Such solicitude for the
visual identity of each member in a building is a
persistent theme in modern architecture.

But out of these respectfully treated structural
units Mackintosh creates – wherever he has
room and opportunity – a kind of interior space
that is undeniably modern; the uprights and
horizontals define space without enclosing it,
much as a pencil line can frame an area of paper
without colouring it. In the justly-celebrated
library of the Glasgow school, with its upper
gallery supported on beams that do not meet the
upright posts until they have gone a foot or
more beyond the balustrade, the parts are not
modern in themselves, being often elaborately
decorated with handicraft techniques, but their
interlace in space offers the beholder a type of

SILENCE

11

The canonical list of who is, and who isn't, a member of the modern movement was effectively established by Nikolaus Pevsner in *Pioneers of the Modern Movement* in 1936 (later editions are titled *Pioneers of Modern Design*) and that canon has not been seriously questioned, only extended a little, by the two works that depend from it in an almost apostolic succession – *Theory and Design in the First Machine Age* (1960, Architectural Press) by the present author, who was a pupil of Pevsner, and *Modern Movements in Architecture*, by Charles Jenks (1973, Pelican) who was a pupil of the present author. They should be read, if possible, in the historical sequence in which they were published.

architectural experience that is unique to the modern movement.

But the decoration, to say it again, is not modern. It is Art Nouveau at its most intensely period, most hypersensitive and most neurotically overworked. It is tolerable today because it is an expression of Mackintoch's intensely period, sensitive and neurotic personality – in some ways he must be compared to Aubrey Beardsley – and because it was conceived by him integrally with the building. If one peeled off the ornament, the bare structure would not be modern architecture but just a lifeless hulk. The Glasgow School is not modern in parts: it is in every part transitional, poised on the threshold of the modern movement.

But it has another claim on the esteem of modern architects. Mackintosh is numbered among the Pioneers of the Modern Movement, as Professor Pevsner termed them in the title of the first edition of the book in which he traced what is, in many ways, an apostolic succession from the great architectural moralists of the mid-nineteenth century, John Ruskin, Viollet-le-Duc and Gottfried Semper. This apostolic succession, the conscious handing-on of the message of a reformed attitude to design, is of vital importance to the concept of modern architecture: if only because there are times and places where modern architecture cannot be defined except as 'what is done by modern architects' and because the modern movement can always be more rigorously defined by naming its members than by attempting to list its methods.

There is no point in formally setting out a family tree at this juncture: indeed, such graphic devices always involve falsification because of the way in which the same man can influence succeeding generations of followers in opposing directions (as Le Corbusier has done), or in the way in which men on opposite sides of the world can keep in touch nowadays without ever meeting one another. But one can indicate the kind of process, the type of relationship by which the apostolic succession was built up. Three of the greatest masters of modern

architecture, though born in different places and differing circumstances, studied under the same master and underwent the same influence for a short but vital part of their formative years: Walter Gropius, Mies van der Rohe and Charles Edouard Jeanneret (who later called himself Le Corbusier) all passed through the office of Peter Behrens as assistants around 1910. Behrens, at that moment, was the hero of progressive German architecture, responsible for the design of everything from factories to sales literature produced by the giant AEG combine; from him these three earnest young men imbibed the doctrine of the architect as universal designer. From the man behind Behrens, the theorist and design-politician Hermann Muthesius, they all seem to have imbibed that faith in the virtues of standardisation that Muthesius pronounced in a lecture given in 1911, and from publications and an exhibition of the epoch in Berlin they acquired an admiration for Frank Lloyd Wright, whose early houses in the Chicago suburbs indicated to them a way out of the transitional condition, which Mackintosh and Behrens never found.

In a movement as small as the modern one then was, this meant that the leadership of that generation in France and Germany, the two key countries, shared many points of common doctrine. And the movement really was small; when Madame de Mandrot, under Le Corbusier's guidance, gathered them together at La Sarraz in Switzerland for the first of the Congrès Internationale d'Architecture Moderne, the result was no mass rally; the modern movement in Europe was barely three dozen men. CIAM retained this atmosphere until well after World War II; the leaders of modern architecture all round the globe were on christian-name terms with one another, and when they met at Bridgewater in 1947, they could still be packed into a couple of buses for an afternoon at Glastonbury Fair.

By then, CIAM was really an elite within the movement, but students flocked from all over the world to congresses like that at Aix-en-Provence to sit at the feet of the masters: the sense of an apostolic succession by personal contact remained. But, also by then, there were all over the world competent modernists no longer sufficiently aware of being reformers to want to join an organisation like CIAM. Modern architecture had matured, become accepted, was the norm – one could say that if it isn't modern nowadays, it isn't architecture any more, but archaeology, cowardice or fancy dress. Governments, both East and West, after forty years of trying to hammer modern into the ground, began to build modern as a matter of pride, an assertion of progressive status. As a result, the band of dangerous radicals who rallied to la Sarraz found they had become an establishment of elder statesmen and retired titular heads of a world-wide empire now so self-sustaining that it is hardly conscious of being an empire, yet every inch of it was captured and colonised by them between 1910 and 1930.

In that heroic age, they created modern architecture with their own hands, and in the next twenty years they, and their direct followers, took it all over the world: Le Corbusier to Latin America, his pupils to Japan, Gropius to England and America, his students and followers to the Commonwealth, where they met Corbusians coming round from the other side. But when they had conquered the world, nothing was ever quite the same again.

The remark of Ed Stone's quoted at the head of this chapter is both wistful and defiant; wistful in remembering the grand old pioneering days when he and Buckminster Fuller were the terrors of Greenwich Village; defiant because he clearly sensed that the pure white image of a new architecture that he revealed to Americans in the design of the Museum of Modern Art had become a tomb, a whited sepulchre in which modern architecture could die.

But, it cannot be too emphatically said, the style that Stone set out to replace or abolish with such designs as his elegant embassy in New Delhi was only a style; it was not modern architecture, whatever he himself may have thought. Many critics and architects in the 1950s went round, like Stone, announcing with

Edward D Stone and Philip Goodwin: *Museum of Modern Art, New York, 1939*

gloomy good cheer that modern architecture was dead, and drawing the wrong conclusions. All that had happened, in fact, was that modern architecture had ceased to be a stylistic teen-ager, and its practitioners were no longer compelled to wear the uniform of their peer-group for fear of expulsion from the gang, demotion from christian-anme status at CIAM. Any discussion of modern architecture must concern itself largely with this period of almost paranoid teenage conformity, when walls were white, windows large, roofs flat, *or else*, just as any biography of someone in his twenties will be somewhat preoccupied with his teens. But the teen-age uniform of modern architecture, the so-called International Style, or White Architecture, nowhere near exhausts the possibilities inherent in its heredity and formation. The next move was not, as many people thought around 1950, simply to put the clock back half a century and write off modern as a mistake; there was no need to go back to the old architecture that was before 1900.

Although the title 'Towards a New Architecture' (Architectural Press paperback) subtly misses the whole point of the book, Frederick Etchells's translation of *Vers Une Architecture* not only did more than anything else to transmit the emotional drives behind modern architecture to the English speaking world, but it also helped to establish it as almost the only piece of architectural writing that can be classed among the 'essential literature of the Twentieth century.'

Paradoxically, the leading modernists never felt that they had really strayed from that old architecture anyhow. Not from its true and eternal principles. It should be remembered that the most famous book ever written by a modern architect is only called, in English, *Towards a New Architecture*. When Le Corbusier first launched it on the world, its title was, quite simply *Vers une Architecture* – towards an architecture, and the qualities of that architecture were established by confronting the technology of the First Machine Age with the architecture of Ancient Greece: the Parthenon, a 1921 Delage and the proposition 'This is how Phidias felt'.

Now it is difficult not to read such an argument in the sense implied by the book's English title: that an architecture that really matched up to modern technology would have to be radically different from any architecture that had gone before. But Le Corbusier's point is not that: what he wants to say is that all the great styles of the past have been the equals of their contemporary technologies, and that when our own architecture matches our own technology then we shall have an architecture as good as the Parthenon. But also – a point that he has made more of in later books – however modern and technological an architecture may be, it still has to house and shelter a race of men who have only grown a few inches taller since pre-history and only a little more intelligent, battling a force of gravity that is substantially the same on the high plains of Tibet or in the depths of Death Valley, drinking water that is still H_2O whether it comes from a spring or a tap, and breathing air that is almost as consistent in composition all over the world. And such an architecture will be viewed and judged by eyes and brains that do not differ significantly from those that looked upon Stonehenge and wondered if that kind of architecture was here to stay.

Eyes that have been trained to look on the Parthenon and Gothic cathedrals will have no real difficulty in looking at modern architecture – particularly since Doric geometrical purity and Gothic structural frankness are continually set up as standards of architectural merit by modern architects. Briefly, modern architecture is like any other architecture only more so: it has more things to say and ways of saying them. If it has given up certain time-honoured visual comforts, such as naturalistic decoration, it is only in order to have its hands free for other things, but it is still basically what it was – functionally, the creation of fit environments for human activities, aesthetically, the creation of sculpture big enough to walk about inside. Great architecture of every period has always blended the aesthetic and the functional into an indissoluble artefact, and in the very greatest architecture they were never at any time separate in the architects' minds. This was true of a simple shed like the Parthenon or a structure as complex as Rheims cathedral; it is true of a structure as complex as the Glasgow School of Art, or as simple as the Climatron in St Louis, or a shed as unlikely as Victor Lundy's inflatable Atomic Energy Pavilion.

The justification of modern architecture, and of this book too, is that – whatever remains changeless from the past – new forms and methods of integrating the aesthetic and practical have emerged in the present century, new modes of vision, new loyalties and new responsibilities in society. Just what is specifically new in the new buildings themselves is not always easy to define. Architects themselves have shifted their emphasis from forms to functions to materials to space concepts and back again. Such subject headings are useful, and they define the topics of the next four chapters, and each in its time has been brought forward as if it were the complete 'explanation' of modern architecture. Yet none on its own can really illuminate what is new and good about modern architecture, and neither their novelty nor their alleged fallibility explains the curious pass in which the movement finds itself at present.

Even the greatest and most complex exponents of modern architecture have been prone to take cover behind these easy simplifications, pleading historical necessity (the age demanded new methods of construction, etc.) probably

Walter Gropius and Adolf
Meyer: *Fagus factory,
Aalfeld, 1911*

Le Corbusier: *Parliament building, Chandigarh, 1959*

Anthony Lumsden (of DMJM): *Century Bank, Los Angeles, 1972*

because that seemed safer than admitting that the pressure for novelty and change (and much else) came from inside the minds of the architects themselves. Rare is the master like Mies van der Rohe who would give a long, detailed and technically impeccable explanation of some unusual feature of one of his buildings and conclude with 'so that was a very good reason for doing this thing . . . Now I explain the real reason why we did it!'

In a powerful sense, modernity lay in the minds of its practitioners, above all in the minds of its creators – that happy few in the bus between Bridgewater and Glastonbury and a handful of absent friends. With their death, that kind of modernity dies too. And for many observers, even well-wishers of the modern movement, what we have known as modern architecture dies also. And for many ill-wishers, or just puzzled bystanders, it now appears that 'the whole modern thing was just a flash in the pan'. Compared to the great styles of the past, modern architecture (if dead) has indeed had a short life if it is measured against say, the four centuries of English Gothic or one hundred and fifty splendiferous years of Italian Baroque. But measured against the other movements of our own time it has proven spectacularly durable. In the portable and literary arts few have managed to beat a ten-year life-span, neither Futurism nor Dadaism lasted half that time as living forces, though Cubism and Surrealism

both just about managed the canonical decade. In a world where art-movements like Pop and Op have evaporated like the morning dew, the style that runs – visually – from Gropius's Fagus factory of 1911 to Le Corbusier's Capitol buildings at Chandigarh and on to the prismatic mirror-glass skyscrapers being built in the US in the early Seventies, is a style to be reckoned with, durable beyond the expectations of our time.

Supposing it is actually dead, that is. Certainly its old masters are no longer in the land of the living, their great style is under corrosive critical scrutiny and their philosophy set at naught by their radical successors. But they do have radical successors . . . and that is what proves that the movement is not dead. The style, yes; the teenage uniform of white walls and flat roofs and oversize windows has gone, and many of the accompanying tenets of belief are now known to be illusions. But the process that produced both has proven to be irreversible, and the radical succession continues. That is why one can say that 'if it isn't modern, it isn't architecture'. What was once a movement *in* architecture is now the movement *of* architecture, and what were once thought to be death-throes are now seen merely as growing pains. But they are the worst growing pains of all – those of learning to accept that one is no longer a teenage tearaway but a fully paid-up adult.

FUNCTION

The new architecture is functional: that is it is developed out of an accurate setting forth of practical demands ...
Theo van Doesburg

For nearly twenty years, modern architecture was often explained as if its forms were absolutely decided by the functions they had to fulfil, and the total form of its buildings by their total register of functions – and this in spite of the fact that most of its great masters had insisted that Functionalism was not enough. Nevertheless, one of the leading justifications for having a new architecture was that new functions had arisen, and old ones had changed. The reader may judge for himself how real was this justification, by trying to enumerate just how many new functions had appeared between the death of Julius Caesar and the invention of the steam engine. The monastery, the church . . . the list is so short, so few new functions had appeared that, in the Renaissance, architecture was able to resume the classical dress of Roman times with only a little letting out of seams and moving of buttons. At some levels of functional performance, this is still true – the sentimental regard for Georgian architecture depends not only on its alleged 'grace and craftsmanship', but also on its ability to go on serving those functions like charity, bureaucracy, culture and sociability which need few mechanical aids.

But with the appearance of even primitive factories, the old architectural garments began to get badly stretched; with the emergence of the railway station, the reformed prison, the elementary school, the Florence Nightingale type of hospital, the elevator office block, the grand hotel, architects were faced with functional problems for which the past was no guide: a grand hotel is not like the hospice of a monastery, it is not even a cross between a hospice and a palace; an office block is not like the scriptorium of a cathedral, it is not even like a cross between a scriptorium and a prison (whatever humorists of the nineteenth century may have implied); not even in combinations and permutations would the old solutions serve. Even while old building materials and old styles of ornament were employed, the new functions compelled the architects of the Steam Age to build in shapes and sizes that the ancients could not have recognised. Without a workable philosophy that integrated aesthetics and

function, Victorian architects – save only a few of genius – failed to make convincing architecture out of their buildings, but they did not fail as disastrously as some functionalist propagandists have maintained. As has been said, what is important is not that they failed, but that they so nearly succeeded.

All the same, they didn't succeed, and what made their failure intolerable to those who had to follow them was that, by the time the twentieth century was old enough to be aware of itself, the old functions were also in transformation. For the first time in two thousand, perhaps four thousand, years, the daily life of western man (and western woman even more so) was being revolutionised. We are only just beginning to realise how profound a revolution it was that overtook domestic life in the Edwardian age, first at the top of the social order, later spreading to other levels in a process that is not yet finished. Architects, directly involved in the processes of daily domesticity, were forced to recognise the results of this revolution earlier than most of the professions or intelligentsia; a suburban house for a motorised family whose numbers are regulated by parental choice, rather than supernatural accident; the servantless house where mother may be a doctor who receives patients for psychiatric consultations; the electric house with radio, telephone, vacuum cleaner, refrigerator and all the rest of it – the house is not what it was, even before the architect has got his hands on it.

It became necessary for architects to reconsider and re-assess the basic theme of their art, the dwelling of Man. Le Corbusier's slogan 'the house – a machine to live in', is a fair measure of how radical that re-assessment could be. Indeed, the machine/house slogan is so radical that it has been much misunderstood, and much misquoted – usually on purpose! What Le Corbusier really meant was two things: one was a house that resembled a machine in being cheap, standardised, well-equipped and easily serviced, like a mass-produced car; *la maison Citrohan* he called it in an admitted pun on the French baby-car of the period. But he also

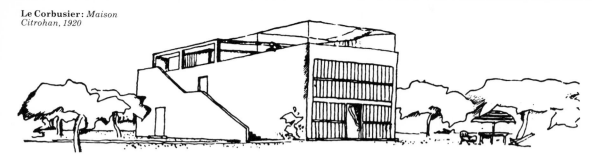

Le Corbusier: *Maison Citrohan, 1920*

meant a house that resembled a machine in being radically well suited to the needs it had to serve, designed with honest – even inspired – rationalism, but without inherited prejudices.

The exigencies of the twenties cheated him of the fulfilment of the mass-production dream, but he had his successes on the other side, designing and sometimes building, a series of houses that were such radical good fits on their inhabitants that it is almost impossible for later, more tradition-bound tenants to live in them.

Yet, at least one of these houses has become a Modern Movement classic, and established something of a new form for domestic architecture. Characteristically, it is in the far suburbs of a capital city, at Poissy, down the Seine from Paris. The house does not see the river, but stands above it in a kind of ideal domestic landscape, a great square of tall grass almost entirely walled in by tall trees (that, at least, is how it was when the house was built: the chances of war and time have wrought miserably with it). Instead of invading, excavating or otherwise monumentalising this perfect setting, the house appears to touch it as little and as lightly as possible, like a helicopter poised for departure. This light stand on the ground is what, typically distinguishes many a modern building from an old one. In many of Richard Wilson's landscape paintings of the eighteenth century we see Palladian houses standing in equally ideal landscapes of uninterrupted lawns framed in trees, but whereas the average English stately home stood broad and heavy on its rusticated basement, Le Corbusier's Villa Savoie at Poissy stands narrow on a few slim columns.

Appears to stand . . . there is quite a lot of house on the ground floor, but it stands well back from the column line and is painted a dark colour so that it tends to disappear. But this is not just an optical trick; between the columns and the ground floor wall, under the square first floor, runs the drive, which – in the original version of the design – came from the main road, turned under the house like a race-track (the curve is preserved in the plan) and then returned, parallel to the run-in, back to the road. Thus, the house began by acknowledging that access by car was the foundation of its existence.

From drive level you ascend by a ramp – which puts the various floors in a different relationship to that implied by a staircase – to the main living floor. Although the ramp rises through the centre of the building, this floor is not, like the *piano nobile* in a comparable villa of an earlier epoch, laid out symmetrically around it. The rooms are arranged round two sides of an open court, and the ramp rises again on one side of the court to reach the roof, as in some Mediterranean peasant houses. All this complicated planning takes place within a regular square box of walls, which tell one nothing about the secret life of the house inside, except that the narrow strip of viewing window that runs all round the house is not glazed when it has open courtyard behind it. The living room which occupies three-quarters of one side of the box and a quarter of the next, opens on to the internal court by way of a floor-to-ceiling window that forms one complete wall of the court, so that the eye travels without interruption from the carpeted floor within to the flagged floor without, even when the sliding window is closed. There is a visual and

Le Corbusier:
*Villa Savoie,
Poissy, 1928–30*

Villa Savoie, the terrace

*Villa Savoie:
plans of ground
and first floors*

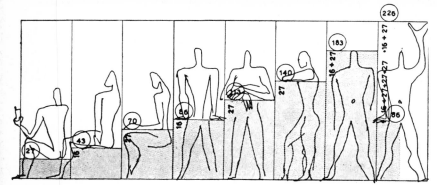

Le Corbusier: 'Modulor' dimensions, 1952

Laszlo Moholy-Nagy has been described as the Johnny Appleseed of modern design, scattering the good word far and wide over Europe and North America. His two seed catalogues are: *The New Vision*, written in 1928 at the end of his Bauhaus years, and *Vision in Motion*, culled from the fruits of his American planting. Exhausted, he burned out and died in 1946, aged fifty-one.

functional ambiguity between what is certainly indoors and what is certainly out, reflecting no doubt, the indoor/outdoor ambiguity of the daily routine of a fashionably sun-loving family of the period, and sun-bathing as such received magnificently its due in the sun-deck on the floor above, sheltered by a loop of walls that make shapes like those in Le Corbusier's paintings, and pierced by a picture-window (the first ever) that frames a scene like a Claude or a Poussin.

This house could not have been built without twentieth century techniques of construction, glass-making, etc., but that is not the point. There would have been no *need* to build it without the twentieth century revolution in domestic life, and it is of crucial importance to an understanding of modern architecture to see how modern architects have shaped up to this revolution that began at home. Basically, they are still serving the same old men as have existed since Neanderthal times, more or less, still breeding, eating, secreting, excreting, sleeping, speaking, hearing, seeing much as they ever did, powered by the same old metabolisms, running at the same old pulse rates.

This familiar old Adam has occasionally been overlooked by architects dizzified and dazzled by advances in technology, but not for long. Le Corbusier has some concept of man pencilled into the corner of his drawings – his *Modulor* system of dimensions was based on the figure of an ideal man – and that most determined of Machine Age enthusiasts, Laszlo-Moholy-Nagy, the Bauhaus philosopher, would sternly remind

his readers that 'Man, not the product, is the end in view' and insist on 'the biological as the guide in everything'. This – in changing interpretations – is the key to the modern architect's view of function and how to design for it.

It may be the same old man, but seen in a changed new light. Moholy's 'biological' is only one of the new aspects of man as he is viewed by sociologists, doctors, psychologists, political theorists, market-researchers, traffic engineers, insurance actuaries, educators, entertainers, city-planners, economists, and everybody else who has any interest at all in making a working estimate of the capacity, needs and performance of *homo sap*. The 'man' of the older cultures was viewed *sub specie aeternitatis*, a tarnished ideal or fallen angel; the man of the culture in which architects have perforce to work nowadays must also be regarded as an observed and annotated man, a sophisticated natural man who can regard himself inside and out through the eyes of an increasingly self-conscious life-style.

Under this double aspect, we can now consider even the design of a functional church. During the teenage period of modern architecture, this would have meant a glass box with an altar at one end, and one or two such were actually built. Yet this is really only a Functional*ist* church, imitating the forms of other, obviously functional buildings such as factories. But nowadays we should mean a building that started from a rigorous analysis of the ritual to be enacted in it, its needs in terms of space, lighting, sight lines and other forms of human contact required by the religion or sect that was to use it, plus processional and other types of access and circulation within or through the 'liturgical room'. It would be the architect's task to work this out from first principles and not accept the habit-bound opinions of priest and congregation, and having found out, to reconcile all these – probably conflicting – requirements in a convincing building. The result is no more likely to be a glass box than it is to be a Romanesque crypt, and the outcome has already been as various as the bulging sail-like curves of Le Corbusier's pilgrimage chapel

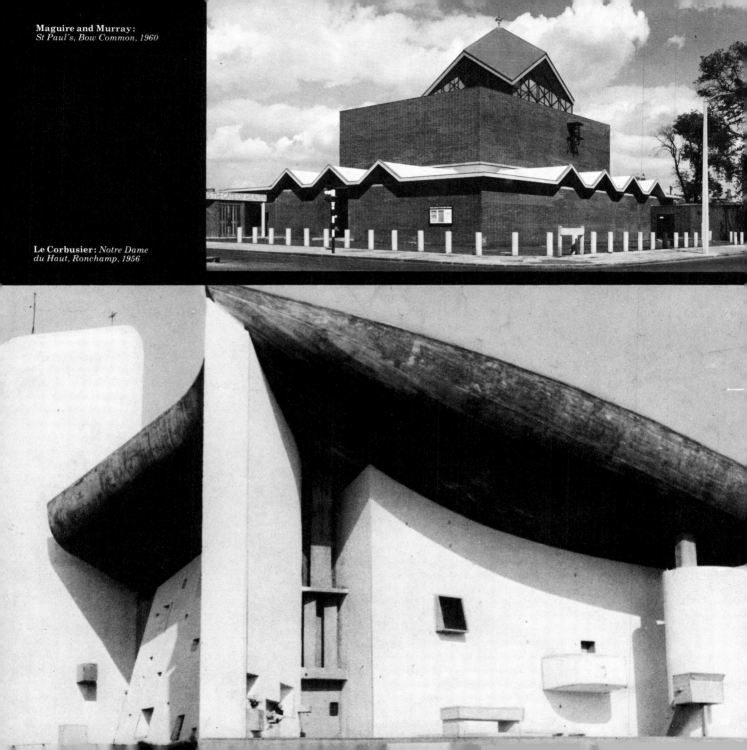

Maguire and Murray:
St Paul's, Bow Common, 1960

Le Corbusier: *Notre Dame
du Haut, Ronchamp, 1956*

at Ronchamp, or the hard-edged brick and concrete angles of Robert Maguire's parish church of Saint Paul, Bow Common.

The essence of the matter seems to be that all functional problems are equal in the eyes of a good modern architect, none are too ancient nor too sacred to be re-examined, none are too trivial or too recherché to be assessed. Surprisingly few of the great modern buildings are dedicated entirely to utterly unprecedented functions, few of the entirely new functions have yet evoked first-rate architecture: there is the incredible Vertical Assembly Building at Cape Kennedy, but where is your masterpiece among atomic power-stations? There isn't one, and this may well be due to the fact that in fields like atomics and weaponry the architect is not allowed to make a radical scrutiny of the problem because some of the information he needs is 'classified'. It is when they have been given, literally, the run of the building that modern architects have made their real contributions to functional improvement in design, as in the British schools that the world soon recognised as one of the achievements of post-war architecture.

This habit of radical enquiry has become so ingrained in the thinking of the major modern architects that they have been able to export their talents as intellectual *agents-provocateurs* into other fields – and not only of design. Most notably, Charles Eames was once retained by a major US industrial concern to interfere in its policy-making activities in other fields besides design, simply because for a man like him no routine or ritual of method and procedure is sacred or beyond investigation. Modern architects, as a profession, take it almost as a given right to apply their talents to any problem that requires solving, and as a result they have left their mark on more than just architecture. Eames, for instance, came to world notice first as the inventor of a family of metal-legged, plastic-bodied chairs that have wrought the second great revolution in furniture design in this century.

The previous revolution in furniture design was

Charles Eames: *chair. 1948*

G. T. Rietveld: *Red/blue chair, 1917*

Marcel Breuer: *chair, 1927*

Mart Stam, born 1896, and **Marcel Breuer**, born 1902, came together in the creative moment that gave the Twentieth Century one of its most characteristic objects, the steel tube chair. They had known one another and their work for a little time before 1927, but after that their paths diverged utterly – Stam to Russia, back to his native Holland, to East Germany, and ultimately to a kind of underground legend as a mystery man whose whereabouts were never precisely known; Breuer to the United States and the position of almost the favourite architect of the progressive establishment, hence his collaboration in the design of the UNESCO building in Paris with Nervi and Bernard Zehrfuss.

also the work of architects: three of them – Mies can de Rohe, Mart Stam and Marcel Breuer – all with a pretty good claim to have invented the resilient steel-tube chair around 1927. One of their contemporaries, who hadn't invented the steel-tube chair but patently wished he had, insisted that the actual facts of authorship were unimportant compared to the 'rationalism' that had 'engendered a collective art'. Rationalism was the supposed mental discipline of the Functionalist epoch, but reason, being only a mechanical system like an electronic computer, can produce no more than has been put into it. You could feed the concepts *sit* and *tube* into a computer for a century (which was about how long mass-produced metal furniture of a sort had been in existence) and nothing radical would come out. It was a series of imaginative assaults on the problem of sitting and the kind of structure that should be associated with it, by the Dutch architect Gerrit Rietveld, without any reference to steel tube, that opened the road toward the modern metal chair.

He enquired how the body sat, and how it could be best supported in that position, and produced a wooden chair in which the surfaces on which the body rested were carefully discriminated from the structure that maintained those surfaces at the right inclination and height from the ground. The result was, in fact, more of a work of art than a fully functional machine for sitting in, but the reasonableness of the solution struck a generation of men like a shaft of light. Yet reason could not have posed the original question; only a well-trained imagination coupled with a habit of taking nothing on trust could have indicated the answer. This training, this habit of mind, are attributes that every great modern architect possesses, that every great modern school of architecture aims to inculcate in its students, and it is the impact of these twin instruments of investigation on the complex of functions old and new that gives modern architecture its peculiar moral authority. Or is it only a *claim* to moral authority? What functions were to be investigated or served? It takes an uncommon

measure of agreement between architect and client before functional problems can even be identified. The ancient conventions of life and leisure that made it possible for clients and architects to agree on a set of functional priorities without even discussing them (everybody knew what the functions of a Georgian country house were) had begun to disintegrate well before the present century began – hence the questioning attitude of modern architects.

Where the clients happened to be men of similar backgrounds to the architects, discussion (at least) could proceed. It was this community of terms of reference that made possible Charles Eames's role as company gadfly at IBM, and it also made possible the rise of modern school architecture in Britain – teachers and architects were innovators of a similar stripe who found ways of communicating profitably with one another. But where the clients were committees of politicians, medical men and others not (alas!) normally open to constructive debate, such communication as took place could be relevant to everything (taxpayers' interests, medical hierarchies, etc.) except the functions that really mattered. It was the problem of designing for the ever-changing functional needs of hospitals that drove one British architect to the proposal that 'the architect should study the client's brief with care, and make sure that he really understands it. Then he should tear it up and find out what the client really wants.' Clients were understandably obsessed with the faults of old hospitals – that was why they were re-building, after all – but simply to correct the faults of an old design is not the best way of producing a new one that is good.

The old design might well have been good of its time, but medical practice has developed at such breakneck speed since the early days of anaesthetics and antisepsis that hospital buildings are often obsolete within five years of construction and through no fault of the architects. But in the rush to serve new and demanding functions, old and ever-valuable ones can get overlooked. The excitements generated by X-rays and iron lungs and dialysis and cobalt bombs can make client and architect alike forget that the only *raison-d'être* of the whole epic of medical progress is still that old Adam of mankind – probably prostrate behind a screen and hoping that a nurse will come with a bed-pan before something unspeakable happens.

In hospital design, the only functional revolution worth the bother has been the perpetual rediscovery of the patient; in schools, of the child. They are the true and ultimate clients of the architect, but they are peculiar clients. They have a legal constituency and in a modern state they must be served, but against this they are the captives of their condition. They do not have the privilege of voting with their feet if they do not approve of the buildings to which a negligently benevolent society has committed them. The ultimate clients of housing, however, expect and usually appear to possess the right to go or to stay as they wish. Furthermore, they expect the accommodation of their choice to produce an environment that relates directly and convincingly to themselves and their way of life. They expect this the more so when their 'choice' is illusory – as it often is, since the 'iron laws of economics' and the monumental ambitions of architects usually combine to provide them with structures too vast and too inflexible ever to adapt to their emotional and cultural needs.

The architect can only aim at a generalised satisfaction of averaged social needs, and that may satisfy nothing. The ultimate clients may then decide to take it out on the building or, worse, on one another. The range of social breakdowns, from indifferent vandalism to violent anarchy, to which some recent housing schemes are prone, has become common knowledge. The blame for such breakdowns should be laid in varying proportions at many doors; managers, commissioning authorities, local politics, builders, deficient welfare services, architects, all play their part. But it is usually the architects who get the public blame and equally usually show an almost masochistic enthusiasm to accept it.

Le Corbusier: *Workers' housing, Pessac, 1926. Do-it-yourself improvements, as of 1967*

Breast-beating is now something of a growth-industry within the architectural profession, and much of it stems from sheer bafflement that the noblest symbol they have contributed to modern society – gleaming new apartments towering over the huddled slums they replace – should after half a century be suddenly set at naught and discredited. Even at a small scale – that of two-storey terraces – there is now doubt that the architect can any longer serve the needs and aspirations of 'just folks' and much has been made of the extensive alterations by the occupiers of the workers' housing at Pessac, near Bordeaux. Its architect? The great Corbusier, no less, and if he could not get it right, who could, sob the breast-beaters.

Come on, now! What proportion of the houses have been significantly altered? Not even half. And how long have they been standing? Half a century. And is it so uncommon for houses to be altered within fifty years of their completion? Corb's record is no worse than any other architect's since the beginning of time. The difference lies in the claims made (and not always by Corb) for the perennial and infallible functional rightness of the designs. If that kind of arrogance of mind has been broken by recent crises of confidence it might be no bad thing. The profession clearly no longer feels that it is uniquely qualified to interpret and then serve the functional needs of others, and this greater humility before the problem of function may yet prove to be one of the great divides between the modern architecture that was and the modern architecture to come . . . a greater divide than between any succeeding fashions in architectural forms.

FORM

... to invent and create
forms symbolising our age
Walter Gropius
**We refuse to recognise
problems of form**
Mies van der Rohe

Auguste Perret: *Garage Ponthieu, Paris, 1906*

The outrageous polemical tones of *Ornament and Crime* and other early propagandist writings in favour of a new architecture, have long been hard to believe and harder to experience in the original. Now, however, many of them – including the Futurist texts – are available in workman-like translations in: Ulrich Conrads, *Programmes and Manifestos on Modern Architecture* (Studio Vista and MIT Press).

The forms of modern architecture are a periodical embarrassment to its practitioners (the contradictory opinions, previous page, were uttered almost simultaneously by men employing identical architectural forms) because they are not much determined by the functions that the buildings have to perform, and not much determined by the materials of which they are constructed. Neither function nor construction is without its influence, and the man who turns with enthusiasm to new functional solutions and new structural methods is likely to turn also to new formal expressions. But to blame these innovations for the new forms of modern architecture is like blaming the saxophone for the sound of jazz, simply because it is an obvious innovation.

What is owed to functional demands is most often the general arrangement of parts – there are a strictly limited number of ways in which a flow-production factory or a main-line rail-terminus can be laid out, and these do, indeed tend to settle the bulk form of the total building. But not conclusively; the choice of one method of construction as against another, which may arise from quite separate considerations, will drastically affect the silhouette of that bulk against the sky, the facade it presents to the street. Ideally, form, function and construction should appear inevitable and indissoluble, and we almost expect the precise solution to be so specifically inevitable to one particular building that we may suspect it when we find it exactly repeated on another; the real criticism of plagiarism in modern architecture is not that modernists over-prize individuality, but that every building is a unique problem in its own setting and circumstances, and deserves a unique solution.

Such unique solutions are felt to be feasible because modern techniques of construction make almost any form possible. A generation that has been brought up to despise the Beaux-Arts proposition that the architect simply dreams up a shape and '. . . later one can show how it may be built; that is, the realisation of something already conceived', has been driven into a similar position by sheer abundance of structural ingenuity. Provided the client can foot the bill, engineers have become able to furnish architects with practically any form they want.

What forms have they wanted, and why? In the first instance they wanted clean simple forms, because all the old styles, and even Art Nouveau, had been complex and ornate. By about 1910 they were ready for someone to tell them that decoration was wrong – only to discover that the words had already been uttered, by Adolf Loos. In a brilliant, muddle-headed and highly Viennese essay entitled *Ornament and Crime*, written in 1908, he argued that ornament is not a fit occupation for a civilised man of the twentieth century, that ornament is a mark of savagery or criminal retrogression, an outlet for depraved sexuality . . . 'as a general rule, one can rank the cultures of different peoples by the extent to which their lavatory walls have been drawn upon'.

By 1914, the pioneer modernists had got the graffiti off their walls, but the walls remained surprisingly similar to most previous walls. In Germany, one Father of the Modern Movement, Peter Behrens, continued to fit industrial functions ingeniously into what were still, in total bulk, Doric temples; in France, the other Father, Auguste Perret, was using reinforced concrete to create a column and beam architecture that was entirely classical in feeling, and classical also in many of its details.

This persistent classicism that the Fathers passed on to the Masters of the next generation is not to be despised; it was the unspoken code of honour that held modern architecture together in the teenage period, and underlay its choice of forms, much as the idea of the gentleman underlies the English idea of elegance.

But while the teenage uniform was being settled, the classical prejudice operated to kill off the first crop of really original forms that the movement produced. From 1912 to 1922 – from Hans Poelzig's water tower in Posen to Eric Mendelsohn's hat factory at Luckenwald –

there flourished in German-speaking countries a school of so-called expressionists who genuinely strove to find new forms for new functions. The last major work of this movement, Hugo Haering's farm at Gut Garkau, was rapidly pushed into the limbo labelled *romantic* by the uniformed conformists of the teenage period, only to emerge again with force and authority as a prophecy of what would happen to one wing of modern architecture in the nineteen-fifties: it could almost be a mature work of Alvar Aalto, grand master of Finnish modernism.

The way in which modern architecture has somewhat circled back on itself is an uncomfortable reminder that the supposedly rational forms of the twenties were quite as much formalist as they were functional in inspiration, and that the history of architectural form in our time has an almost independent

development. Outside the classical tradition of the profession itself, those forms of the twenties had three linked sources in the traditions of modern fine art. And although those sources worked differently on different architects, the end product was a remarkable unanimity of manner in the International Style, between 1926 and 1946.

One of these three sources has had a devious and underground effect: Futurism, with its sweeping messianic enthusiasm for 'the machine'. A literary movement in its origin, with extensive ramifications into the visual arts, it taught a generation to look for inspiration in the technology of the First Machine Age, and exalted certain forms and materials as being proper to a Machine Age art. Though spiritually bankrupt by the end of the first world war, its passing unmarked by any architectural monuments worthy of the name, its relevance

Peter Behrens: *AEG Turbinenfabrik, Berlin, 1908*

Hans Poelzig: *water-tower,*
Posen, 1910

Erich Mendelsohn: *factory,*
Luckenwald, 1923

Alvar Aalto: *civic centre,*
Saynatsalo, 1952

Hugo Häring: *farm*
buildings, Garkau, 1923

33

Antonio Sant' Elia: *generating station, 1913*

Le Corbusier: *Villa Cook, Boulogne-sur-Seine, 1926*

J. J. P. Oud, born in 1890, was conspicuous in the twenties; he was the first to reveal, in any substantial body of work, the temper, preoccupations and preferred architectural forms of the budding International Style. With van Doesburg he was one of the founders of the *Stijl* group in 1917, but its aesthetic extremism soon repelled his craftsmanly mind, and he was one of the first to resign. Drifting further and further away from his fellow modernists, he died, ignored or execrated in 1963.

to the true line of development of modern architectural form is shown in the astonishingly prophetic sketches of one of Futurism's fringe-members, Antonio Sant'Elia, which frequently anticipated the forms of the twenties.

But, more important than this, Futurism survived into the twenties as a buried moral imperative, giving power and conviction to forms drawn from the other two sources, Cubism and abstract art. From Cubism's wandering emphasis on the regular geometrical solids (canonised by Cézanne as the cylinder, sphere and cone and thus belonging to a tradition that goes back to Plato) come a group of forms, mostly cubic and rectangular, but including also cylinders and half-cylinders (handy for staircases). These forms were realised, where humanly possible, in absolute Platonic purity; cornices, cappings, sills, dripstones were rigorously suppressed, even the facts of structure were plastered over and rendered smooth to give a homogeneous surface and preserve the uninterrupted purity of the form.

This last practice, of course, makes quiet nonsense of slogans like truth to materials (the public is so confused that it believes these plastered surfaces are really reinforced concrete) and is most commonly perpetrated by Le Corbusier and the French wing of Modernism, but the most extensive justifications of it on purely formal grounds, are to be found in the writings of J. J. P. Oud, the Dutch architect (another pre-1914 pupil of Peter Behrens) who is more generally associated with the influence of abstract art on architecture. This movement, descended from both Cubism and Futurism, filled a desperate gap in the architectural thought of Holland, Germany and Russia immediately after the First World War. Form-hungry architects fastened on the work of Malevitsch, Lissitsky, Mondriaan and van Doesburg, and extracted from it a repertoire of rectangular forms and a set of rules of protocol for introducing them to one another. In this they were energetically assisted by the artists themselves, who believed that their art had immediate architectural relevance. Both Lissitsky and van Doesburg were active

propagandists, and the latter ran a magazine under the title of *de Stijl*, that helped to make the abstract art movement aware of itself at an international level.

Nevertheless, that internationalism ran only on a line from Amsterdam to Moscow at first and left France untouched. Le Corbusier's work – say, the villa Cook – in 1926 is not very like one of Mies van der Rohe's works of the same period, such as his monument to the Communist martyrs Karl Liebknecht and Rosa Luxembourg. Yet a year later the French and German schools, Cubist and abstract, had fused into a single style. For a stirring moment at the Weissenhof exhibition of 1927, they stood before the world united in forms and intentions; the show houses designed by Gropius, Oud, Mies, Le Corbusier and others were so much of one mind that Alfred H. Barr coined the term *International*

Mies van der Rohe (planner): *Weissenhof Exhibition, Stuttgart, 1927*

Mies van der Rohe:
*monument to Karl Liebknecht
and Rosa Luxembourg, 1926*

Kasimir Malevitch:
*Fundamental Suprematist
Elements, 1914*

Costa, Niemeyer, Reidy and
others: *Ministry of
Education, Rio de Janeiro,
1943*

Style to describe it.

Poised for world conquest, the new architecture discovered that it had a uniform by which friend could be distinguished from foe, a uniform whose adoption indicated that its wearer wanted to be considered as one of the gang. For twenty years – thirty in the case of some critics – the defence of modern architecture was the defence of that uniform quite as much as the defence of Functionalism, and there are still people today who cannot accept a building as functional unless it wears the uniform gear.

But already in the early thirties, Le Corbusier was adjusting his dress, and incorporating sporting or tweedy elements not accepted by the rest of the gang. At Mathés, on the Biscay coast, he built a little holiday house with pitched roofs and random masonry walls and rough carpenter's woodwork. Romantic, the critics decided between alarm and admiration, while Le Corbusier himself went off to South America, there to inspire in Brazil a group of young (or youngish) architects to creat the first *national* style of modern architecture. From Lucio Costa's Ministry of Education in Rio, obviously Corb-inspired, to Oscar Niemeyer's government buildings in the all-new capital city of Brasilia, this style has been the envy of the world – and played havoc with the forms of the teenage uniform. It has kept the tall slab shapes, often raised on stilts in the Corbusian manner, it has kept the smooth surfaces – sometimes – and the simple geometry – when it feels like it – but it has carried them all to a degree of freedom so marked and so personal that the Italian critic Gillo Dorfles has, with some justification, termed it Neo-Baroque.

All this was implicit in Le Corbusier's own style, anyhow, as his later work in India will testify. Wihout quoting ancient forms, nor betraying his own modern forms, he achieved a huge, grave, personal rhetoric in works like the Parliament Building in Chandigarh that can be compared to his own description of Michelangelo's work on St. Peter's Rome, **'Gigantic geometry of harmonious relationships . . . the mouldings are of an intensely passionate character, harsh and pathetic'** – except that

Le Corbusier: *holiday house, Mathés, 1935*

House at Mathés, balcony

Corbusier achieved that character without using any mouldings, because he was a committed modernist. All that has happened to modern architecture since the International Style broke up is that different schools and different individuals have pursued aspects and possibilities of the style to their logical-illogical conclusions. The Brazilians went one way; Mies van der Rohe and his followers went another, driving the narrow logic of frame construction to a condition where his followers have given US big business a uniform as correct, well-cut and standardised as a Brooks Brothers suit. Others again, stimulated by the emergence of great engineers like Pierluigi Nervi or Felix Candela have brought the Modern Movement's long-ingrained admiration of engineers out into the open as frank imitation of their forms: sincere flattery indeed, though often with insufficient knowledge of constructional maths to ensure that these forms can be built as they have been designed.

In all these developments one thing is certain: that they are outgrowths of the International Style. Sensing an excess of refinement, some young and not-so-young architects have tried to back out of this formal free-for-all, and recapture virtues they feel to be mislaid today. Some merely revived the shapes and details of primitive Modernism – the Neoliberty movement, or Art Nouveau Revival in Italy as an example – and some tried to recover the heroic stance and dogmatic certainty of an earlier day – the New Brutalists in England in the 1950's.

Out of all this there emerges a situation where an irregular almost windowless brick box, a lattice dome covered with transparent plastic, or a square tower of tinted glass, will all be recognised as modern *by their forms* – pretty much as the family likeness of French, Norwegian and Greek will be recognised by a student of languages. What these various manifestations of modern have in common is not easy to put into words, though a smattering acquaintance with modern architecture will soon begin to suggest affinities to an observant eye. Their minimum common property is that

they are not like any forms in the architecture that was before 1900. Their first positive property in common is that they all have parallels, however devious, with the other plastic arts of their common period. The next is that they take extreme advantage of new constructional materials, and new constructional techniques; in the extended sense that where brickwork appears in an unmistakably modern context, it is not walling built according to the rule of the bricklayer's practised thumb, but apt to be calculated brickwork, treated by the same kind of slide-rule disciplines as prestressed concrete or extruded aluminium. If new materials have not been altogether decisive in determining the forms of modern architecture, new ways of thinking about structure lie very close in places, and it is now time to examine the relationship of thought and material in modern construction.

CONSTRUCTION

... with raw materials to
construct moving
relationships
Le Corbusier

Auguste Perret: *Notre Dame le Raincy, 1923*

In Paris in the early twenties it was possible to talk as if modern architecture had been caused by reinforced concrete. Certainly there was some exciting concrete-work to be seen, but Auguste Perret's concrete church of Notre Dame du Raincy was hardly modern, and Freyssinet's heroic hangars at Orly were hardly architecture. As far as buildings that could be called modern architecture were concerned, there was no concrete to be seen at all: surfaces were neatly rendered and painted over to conceal the fact that the concrete often had to share the structure with cinder blocks, pot tiles or even – save the mark! – bricks. The budgets on which pioneer modern buildings were constructed were commonly too tight to admit of any larking about with untried materials or experimental constructional techniques and even where finance permitted them, local building regulations, usually didn't. Modernity lay in the functional planning, the forms of the exterior, and was spread thinly over the surfaces to conceal the unmodern materials of which the structure was so often built.

Why this sensitivity about materials, the desire to make the house look modern-built? In Holland, W. M. Dudok successfully combined the forms of modernity with brick surfaces; the result was a rave success in the middle-of-the-road countries like England, but universally execrated among convinced modernists, clearly because they felt that brick was in itself a betrayal of the aims of the modern movement. It was, of course, an offence against the clean-wall orthodoxy deriving from Adolf Loos's bent puritanism, but it was rarely combatted on those terms – it was the idea of a solid load-bearing wall that was abhorrent, and it was always construction, not aesthetics, that formed the hub of controversy.

The reasons were complex. One of them is embedded deep in the history of the idea of modern architecture. Early in the new century, Hermann Muthesius drew attention to the splendours of the constructional masterpieces of Victorian engineering, such as the Crystal Palace and the Eiffel Tower, and bade his followers pay attention to them. Twenty-five years later, Sigfried Giedion's book *Bauen in Frankreich* resumed the theme and extended it to cover more recent work in reinforced concrete as well as the earlier work in iron. But he also drew direct parallels between the early masterpieces of engineering and the work being done by his own friends and contemporaries, implying some similarity of method or intention. This was gratifying, because it gave the new-fledged International Style a reputable ancestry; but how real was it?

Psychologically, it was real enough – the whole generation was abnormally sensitive to the aesthetics of engineering work, and most held the *Grands Constructeurs* of the previous century in genuine esteem. Furthermore, they were attached emotionally to engineering materials by a tradition extending from the Futurists, who had praised steel, concrete, glass, plastics, lightweight and impermanent materials, and damned bronze, marble and other monumental stuff; Le Corbusier spoke in this tradition when he praised aircraft as 'little houses that fly and yet can resist tempests'. Associated with the tradition at this point is the mystique of prefabrication that gripped most

of the masters of that time, the mass-produced house made in a factory out of lightweight modern materials. Some of the prestige of such a structure was felt to rub off on other structures built, or even appearing to be built, out of the same materials.

Willem Marinus Dudok: *Town Hall, Hilversum, 1928*

Behind this again lurks the mystique of the engineer as the noble savage of the machine age: a mystique owed partly to Adolf Loos (like so many radical myths of our time) who always admired what he believed to be unselfconsciousness in design, and partly to the Futurist Movement (like so many more of our myths) who professed to see in engineers the outlines of an alien culture 'the gift of mechanical prophecy, the flair for metals'. By the early twenties, Le Corbusier was giving engineers the full noble savage treatment, 'healthy and virile, active and useful, balanced and happy in their work'. Modified over the years, some version of this proposition has always persisted since, and even when architects fear and envy engineers who threaten to take away their work, they are still prepared to admire to distraction any engineer whose work seems moderately sympathetic to them.

Le Corbusier's circle admired Freyssinet, without showing the slightest desire to employ his forms or his methods; the contemporary *G*-group in Berlin admired Matte-Truco's super-Futurist car-factory at Turin with a race-track on its roof. The followers of Sigfried Giedion in the thirties admired the bridges of the Swiss engineer Robert Maillart, while the first generation of outright modernists in Britain could find no praise too high for the work of the engineer Owen Williams. After the war, a growing wave of admiration for the vaultwork of Pierluigi Nervi was the prelude to a cult of engineers such as modern architecture had not seen before, and the cult did not lack cult-objects and heroes – after Nervi came Torroja, Catalano, Buckminster Fuller, Defaille, Frei Otto and a host of others.

By this time, the part played by the engineers in determining architectural form was real. Influential sections of the Modern Movement around 1950 were in the mood for a revolt against the rectangular rectitude of the teenage uniform; the emergence of a new generation (*sic*: Fuller was in his fifties) advocating a new principle of construction (*sic* again: the vault, almost as old as architecture) was the vital

45

Burnham and Root:
Monadnock block, Chicago, 1892

François Hennebique:
villa, Bourg-la-Reine, 1904

Auguste Perret: *house in rue Franklin, Paris, 1903*

Auguste Perret did not invent concrete, nor was he alone in his generation in making pioneering use of it in architecture, because there were other great French constructors – Hennebique, Freyssinet – who made equal contributions to the rise of reinforced concrete technology. What Perret achieved in a career that spans from 1890 (he was born in '71) to 1954 was to establish concrete as a respectable architectural material in its own right, neither a substitute nor a subterfuge. Reading: Peter Collins, *Concrete, the vision of a new architecture* (Faber 1959).

coincidence and the Modern Movement has been in uproar ever since. But there really was something new in the situation, however – the application of new techniques of thought to curved structures had at last made a mass breakthrough.

In earlier days, Freyssinet, Maillart, Nervi, had made only tentative and marginal assaults on the problem of vaulting, but they and their contemporaries had begun to accumulate a body of experience, to which the application of radical methods of tensioning the reinforcement in concrete shells, and the application of radical geometrical techniques in built-up structures, came as the last liberating gesture. There followed a revolution that appears to be more profound than that brought on by the first discovery of reinforced concrete or framed construction.

The freedoms originally brought to architecture by reinforced concrete and metal framing had less to do with the ability to project cantilevers etc., than with reducing the mass of supporting structure at ground level. Columns could be slighter and further apart, thick supporting walls were no longer necessary. These advantages were not essential to the creation of large buildings serving modern functions – as witness the tall Monadnock office block in Chicago, entirely in load-bearing masonry. Nor did architects at once scramble to secure the advantages that framed structure could offer, not until a variety of other influences had altered their aesthetic outlook. The house that François Hennébique built for himself in 1904 as a demonstration of the potentialities of concrete looks humorous rather than prophetic because its style is so gauche and disorganised, whereas Auguste Perret's block in the rue Franklin looks far more convincing, in spite of its less adventurous construction, because it has about it a whiff of the new aesthetic and a genuinely radical plan; required by town-planning laws to make a light well through the block, Perret put it on the front instead of the back, giving all rooms views across the Seine, instead of making half of them look into a cramped courtyard.

In other words, when a new kind of form and a new kind of plan were wanted, the constructional means were there to achieve them, the means being a steel or concrete frame, with its narrow supports and wide spans, its ability to stand narrow on the ground, straddle roads, send out cantilevers and accept any sort of skin from solid stone to transparent glass or even nothing at all – at the top of Perret's block the frame suddenly erupts, free and unencumbered, into two little loggie.

The second structural revolution was of the same order, only more so. Vaulting suddenly

Max Berg: *Jahrhunderthalle, Breslau, 1913*

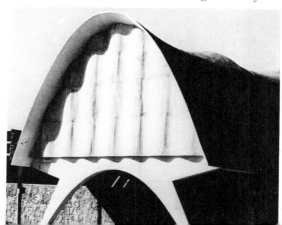

Felix Candela: *Cosmic Ray Pavilion, Mexico University, 1953*

Felix Candela, commonly thought a native Mexican genius, because all his known work is in that country, was born in Madrid in 1910, and left Spain only after the Civil War. Even then, it was not until the very late Fifties that he turned definitively to the theory and practice of lightweight shell-vaulting in concrete.

became easy – there is no other way to express it. The last great vault of the experimental period had been Max Berg's superlative *Jahrhunderthalle* of 1913 in Breslau, massive, monumental, profoundly exciting but far too solid in its members to look easy. The vault that opened the second revolution was not massive, nor monumental. Felix Candela's Cosmic Ray Pavilion for the University of Mexico is no bigger than most houses, and its smallness was part of the attraction. It could be visualised as part of a larger structure, the quantities of materials and labour were such as could be encompassed in a passing thought – a few builders trowelling on a couple of truckloads of cement by hand – the formwork was ordinary old planks of wood, and the designer was reputed to have done the maths in his head.

At the same time, the ability of other simple materials to produce sophisticated structures was being demonstrated in Milan, where, at the Tenth Triennale, there were shown two of Buckminster Fuller's domes made of sheets of carboard cut and scored, for all the world like making up the models on the back of cereal packets, joined together with something for all the world like an ordinary office stapler, and covered by a membrane for all the world like a domestic polythene bag. Yet it is Candela's shuttering that really marks the epoch, because it had always been the argument from shuttering that was the last ditch defence of the rectangular framed structure which – literally – supported the rectangular uniform of teenage modern. Because concrete had to be poured in wooden moulds, which were cheapest to make from straight planks, concrete would be square, even if it performed better in mult-curved vaults, because curved shuttering was ruinously

expensive to set up. But now Candela showed that by picking the right geometric form – such as a hyperboloid, called a 'ruled form' because it was generated by straight lines – you could get complex three-dimensional curves out of simple plank shuttering. So far this dramatic extension of the powers of the plain piece of wood was applied only via the hyperboloid family: the warped slab, the hyperboloid of rotation and the hyperbolic paraboloid, but there are so many of them that their end was never in sight. In addition, they are mostly structurally sound: that familiar hyperboloid of rotation, the cooling tower, is a case in point, so that they cannot be brushed off as mere formalist whimsy.

Be it also noted, that these unexplored extensions of structural possibility have been caused by thinking, not new materials. The amount of life in the old materials is extraordinary: concrete is fighting back with all sorts of new pre- and post-tensioning systems, as well as in lightweight forms; wood in laminates, boards, and built-up beams, as well as in panels where it is associated with metals and plastics; new methods of structural analysis – like the plastic theory – have given new life to steel framing. All this before we even begin to consider plastics as such. This class of materials, however, still seems to be languishing in the condition of concrete before Auguste Perret: outside the unpredictable field of inflatables, it is looking for a master who will give it form, and the only real candidate so far has been Ionel Schein, another hero of the mass-production dream. It has been suggested that the forms of plastics are being invented elsewhere in another material – by Le Corbusier's later work in concrete, for instance – and if that is so, the old rationalist dogma about technique dictating form will have to be pensioned off for good. It has done the Modern Movement good service as a creative myth, but new materials no longer serve to explain what is new about modern architecture. Neither brick nor fibreglass account for the modern architect's radical attitude to function, nor do they inhibit him in applying it; neither steel nor concrete account for, and neither is necessary to, the modern architect's radical conception of space.

Schein, Coulon, Magnant: *motel cabin prototype, 1956*

Buckminster Fuller: *cardboard dome, Triennale di Milano, 1954*

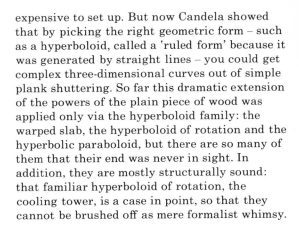

SPACE AND POWER

The experience of space is
not a privilege of the gifted
few, but a biological
function
Moholy-Nagy

Picasso: *Girl with the Mandoline, 1911*

Boccioni: *Bottle Evolving in Space, 1912*

The one thing that is undeniably new about modern architecture is the conscious manipulation of space. We talk loosely about Baroque space and Gothic space and argue about whether the Greeks ever had any sense of space at all; but the ability even to utter the phrase 'architectural space' is an achievement of the late nineteenth century, and a critic's term, or an historian's in the first place. For an architect to think of himself as using or working in space is purely twentieth-century, and one of the things that mark the modern architect over and above any considerations of formal style. But, in addition to this primary cast of mind, the space in which the modern architect consciously works is unlike the space, conscious or otherwise, of any previous architecture.

For most of history, space has existed only inside structures – outside was only nature, chaos, the unmeasurable. Nothing shows this better than the dull exteriors and splendid interiors of Roman baths, or the way that Gothic masons drove stone structure to its logical and unreasonable conclusions in order to create interiors of tremendous height and grace – all that fretwork on the outside was just scaffolding. Renaissance men reversed the process, and could see the outsides of their buildings – as the Greeks did – as isolated works of art. Unlike the Greeks they contrived small, boxy, perspective-centred spaces around them, but those spaces were interiors, closed in by the facades that flanked the piazza, spaces furnished by the buildings they contained.

Baroque space admitted of infinity – perhaps, but we must be wary of reading Baroque mathematics into Baroque planning without good warrant. But this infinity was more usually symbolised than admitted: symbolised by the obelisk that focused the vista, the light falling on the altar at the end of a dark nave. And this was infinity counted from zero at an observer standing in the right place – once you stray from the portico that commands the avenue, the entrance on the axis of the church, any possible relationship with infinity evaporates.

In the nineteenth century, Baroque planning

concepts were stretched to breaking; with the aid of a railway ticket you could travel in a day far beyond the limits of any conceivable architectural composition, and spatial infinity began to be detached from any conceivable view or vista. Physical distance shrank decade by decade, and when a real man could wager to circle the globe in eighty days the roundness of the world became more nearly tangible than when Puck offered to girdle it in forty minutes. When Lindberg flew on schedule from New York to Paris, continental togetherness had arrived, and the world became, in Buckminster Fuller's radical intuition, a single land-mass at the bottom of an ocean of air.

Infinity had begun to enter the consciousness of plastic artists a little before this, around the time that the avant-gardists of all sorts began to acquire the habit of talking of space-time and the fourth dimension. By 1911–12, the Cubist painters of Paris, casually dropping fragments of Einsteinian jargon, were painting pictures whose space, though far from infinite, was not focussed on the perspective conventions of a fixed vanishing point and an ideal viewing point. A picture like Picasso's *Girl with the Mandoline*, has no vanishing point and its shallow space is equally convincing from any viewpoint, near or far, so long as it is somewhere in front of the picture. About the same time, the Italian Futurists, twitting the Cubists for slack terminology, were thinking of space as being focussed by the objects in it, almost irrespective of any observer. For them, space was the interpenetrating spheres of influence of adjacent objects. Somewhere between these two concepts, of an even and unfocussed space, however limited, and an infinite space defined by the matter in it, the basic space concept of modern architecture sppeared, first formulated by Dutch and Russian abstract artists, but built by Frenchmen like Le Corbusier quite as much as any Germans.

In this concept, space is firstly infinite, and extends unrestrainedly in all directions (though it is not in practice handled as if its upward and downward extensions were of great interest). Secondly, this space is measured, defined, made apprehensible by some sort of invisible structure or geometry. Usually, this mental structure is rectangular, and architecture is conceived almost as a kind of three-dimensional cross-word, with some squares filled in, some left blank, some of the lines between them thickened up. In some of Le Corbusier's most sophisticated works, like the Villa Savoie, the structure keeps bursting into view, in the form of columns rising awkwardly in the middle of the room, or just clear of the wall (the same thing also happens in Mies van der Rohe's work around 1930). These columns are part of the regular structural form, they represent the geometric order of space; the walls are inserted *ad hoc*, they represent the architect's free play with and upon that space.

Rectangularity, though, is not a pre-requisite. When entering one of Buckminster Fuller's domes for the first time, one receives a most emphatic sensation of space, modern space, if not square space. But all his domes do possess a very regular and emphatic structure, which gives a powerful sense of being caged in a pervasive geometry, and they often have a translucent covering which admits light, and thus implies space, evenly from all directions.

But, thirdly, the space of modern architecture is conceived as having a very special relationship to the observer: either he, or it, is in motion (in an age that thinks much about relativity, it doesn't much matter which moves). This concept is more allegorical than physical, but its psychological reality is vital to modern architecture. In one way, the interior spaces of a building are to be experienced as a series of partitions of infinite space by an observer moving through them on a prescribed route – *route* is the very word used by Le Corbusier in connection with the ramps of the Villa Savoie – indicated by stairs, platforms, ramps, even the pattern or texture of the floor, which guide him through a series of spatial manoeuvres. Perhaps the best example of this in England is provided by the foyers of the Festival Hall; in America, by the ramps of the Guggenheim Museum.

The opposite case of space moving from, or

Frank Lloyd Wright:
Guggenheim Museum, New York, 1959, interior space

52

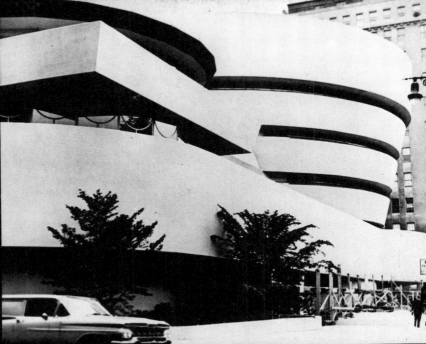

Guggenheim Museum

London County Council Architect's Department: *Royal Festival Hall, foyers, 1951*

53

Gustave Eiffel: *the Eiffel Tower, Paris, 1889*

round, a still observer is not altogether removed from the preceding one in physical fact, but its metaphysical content is more subtle. It has been with us as a working concept ever since the masters of the twenties introduced the idea of the interpenetration of inner and outer space, house and garden. Space in this sense flows almost tidally, away from the observer – when he is outside the house, space flows in, when he is within, space flows out into the garden. That space flows away from the observer can be taken as axiomatic: he is the source of spatial experience. It is also pretty well axiomatic that it flows along a discernible route, and flows out of sight. Space, in modern architecture, does not flow from the centre of a simple square room – there one experiences only a still 'Renaissance' space. It flows round corners, over the edges of balconies, along corridors, up some staircases but not all, and round and behind obstacles and free-standing objects of all kinds.

The epitome of all this kind of spatiality is probably Mies van der Rohe's Farnsworth House, outside Chicago. Space exists here between two given planes, the floor slab and the roof slab, and has no upward or downward extensions whatsoever, except that some sensitive spirits feel that it flows down the four little steps from the floor slab to the terrace.

These two limiting slabs are also the only opaque surfaces on the exterior of the house, everything else is floor to ceiling glass, or nothing at all. As a result the interior space is in almost total communication with the infinite space outside, visually speaking – so much in communication with infinity that some visitors feel a sense of risk from stepping off the edge of the floor-slab.

Between the upper and lower slab there are no visible connections, except the six regularly spaced uprights of the structure which contain an implication of extending beyond the roof slab, so that – allegorically speaking, and viewed from outside – there are some hints of vertical extension into infinity. But only hints: the dominant visual function of those verticals

Joseph Paxton: *Crystal Palace, London, 1851*

is to establish the regular rhythm that measures, controls, the pieces of infinite space that has been marked off to form the house. The only other vertical member that reaches from floor to ceiling is a free-standing construction that functions as a fireplace on one side, and as a kitchen unit on the other, and this is an almost text-book example of the kind of object around which space most persuasively flows, an effect that is amply aided – as in many of Mies's works – by the evident continuity of the floor surface.

This may be the epitome, and a small masterpiece of modern space, but it is not a *great* masterpiece of modern space. The two great masterpieces both antedate the modern movement completely. One was the old Crystal Palace, built out of repetitive glass and iron units for the Great Exhibition of 1851. It was archaic, primitive, but it was so big that it seemed to contain infinity within itself, the space running off endlessly as far as the eye could see, measured off by the regular module of the structure till it flickered away in an optical haze compounded of distance and light. If that was archaic, the mature masterpiece of modern

space, vast, overwhelming, mocking everything that has been put up since, is the Eiffel Tower. Here, every variety of modern spatial experience, plus some more that are unique to the tower, is piled on the viewer in such abundance that he begins to feel insecure and disorientated. Here is participation in infinity, the more convincing because of the great heights involved; here is space that flows away behind structure and spills down stairways; here is space through which the observer moves, either under his own power, or by a variety of different sorts of lifts.

But underlying all, and more fantastic than all, is the structure of the Tower itself, the geometry that controls all spaces. No simple system of regular horizontals and verticals, this great space frame, constructed to battle the wind rather than gravity (Eiffel was one of the pioneers of wind-tunnel testing) occasionally supports a horizontal surface – as a concession to human weakness, one feels – but is, in itself, a system of interlacing diagonals bracing main members that sag not towards the earth's centre, but towards the horizon. Nothing else on earth gives so powerful a sensation of being in free space, free of any reference to the gravity-dominated structures of all other architectural space. Even on the substantial staircases that thread through the lower legs of the structure, an observer feels no sure faith that gravity will go on acting in the same direction after he has turned the next landing; space seems to extend in all directions, globally, indiscriminately around him. It will probably all seem very dull and old hat to men who have actually experienced free fall in outer space, but, as we stand, this old masterpiece offers the earth-bound tourist the surest preview he can have of the spatial experiences of his descendants.

To stand on this ninety-year-old staircase, and experience this free crazy space, is to know something essential about modern architecture. It has grown up, thrown off its teenage uniform, but it still has not equalled the achievement of this pioneer space-machine that is older than a lot of the architects practising today. Modern

architecture, then, has not yet drawn all the dividends on the capital of spatial, structural, formal and functional concepts that were invested for it before birth, let alone the compound interest of new ideas and new techniques that has accrued to it since.

One of the reasons why it has not fully exploited all these legacies may be that there is at least one of them it has never really understood. So little understood that it is actually reflected in a fault in the construction of this book – Form, Function, Materials, Structure and the like having been constituent parts of all known architectures since the beginning of time. So has Space, yet it seems we have a genuinely new awareness of it, as set out in this chapter. Since awareness can only come from experience, have we begun to experience it in a new way too?

Modern art says we have, and has shown us how to. So has the common electric light-bulb, to a stunningly greater degree than modern art has. It enables us to see buildings after dark and to see in dark places in buildings and to see buildings as volumes of light in the dark. Lights have long been set in the windows of buildings, but there is a firmament of difference between a single flame pinpointing the dark bulk of an inscrutable silhouette against the night sky, and the light that floods from a glass-walled office-block or school, revealing its interior life, its structure and its immediate surroundings. In this, modern architecture comes into its own by fulfilling a deep ancestral dream of mansions of light, and at the same time reveals a new way of making space habitable and space perceptible. To achieve this takes more than just light. It takes enormous quantities of light, perhaps fifty times as much per head as we had a century ago. For analagous reasons it also takes heating, ventilating and air-conditioning, mechanically operated elevators and electronic communications. Rehearse in your mind the way in which modern buildings are used day by day, and you will see that there ought really to have been a chapter in this book headed 'Power and light', for Modern Architecture consumes energy like no architecture before it, and one of its worst faults is that it consumes it so

Albert C Martin and
Associates: *Water and
Power Building, Los Angeles,
1963*

Philip Johnson: *Johnson house, New Canaan, Connecticut, 1949*

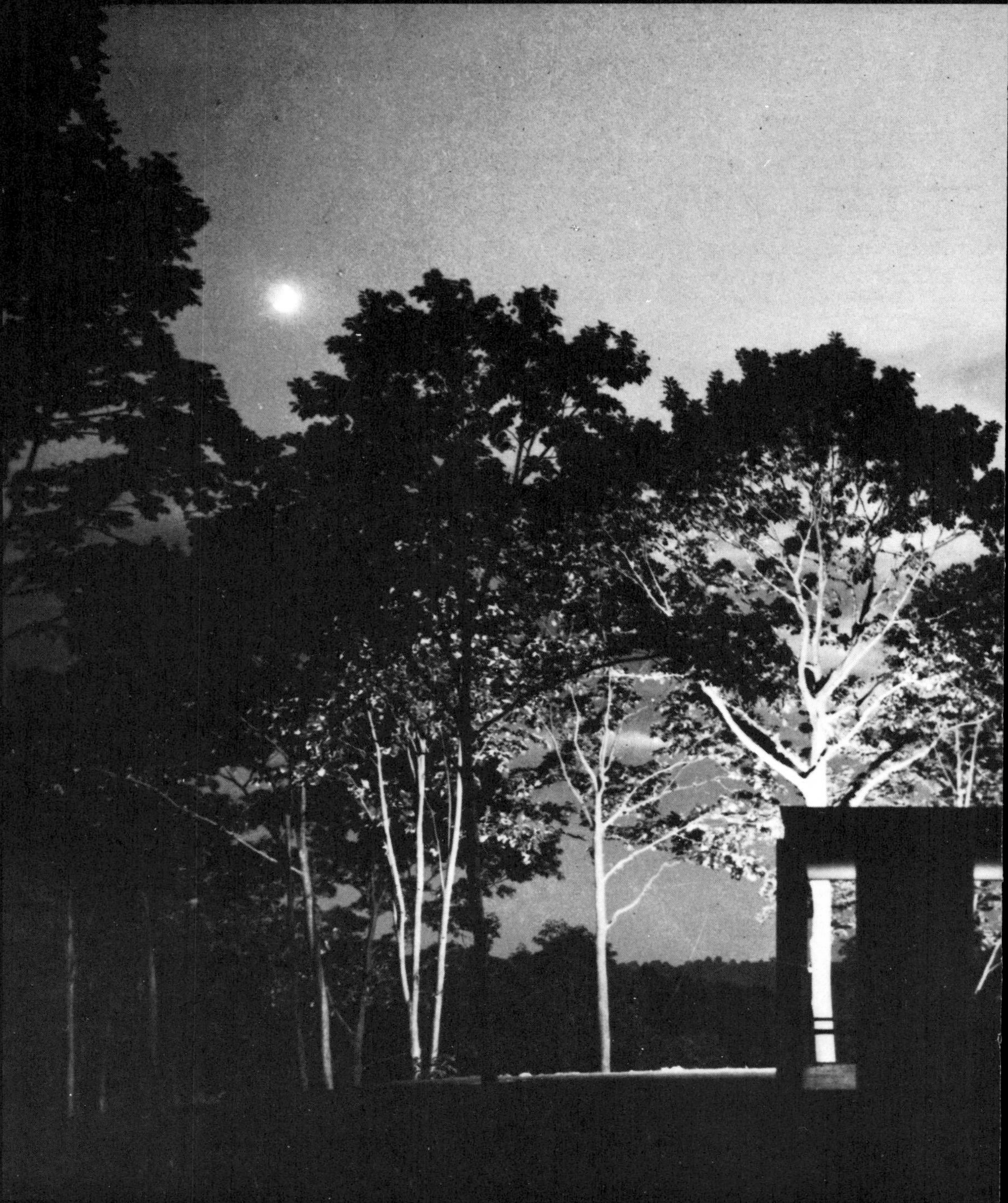

Fremont Street, *Las Vegas,*
Nevada, 1964

negligently. The negligence lies not only in its
frequent wastefulness, but also, and this is
harder to forgive, in its failure to exploit the
architectural possibilities to anywhere near the
full.

The supposedly careless architecture of popular
pleasure has often showed far greater awareness
of these possibilities than has the serious
architecture of cultural purpose. Decades ago the
great movie palaces transformed themselves by
draping their structures in neon and lights.
More recently the casinos of Las Vegas revealed
that with enough light one could almost
abandon structure. The spaces of that wild city
tend to be defined by masses of light that often
have no building around them or behind them.
It may sound strange, almost blasphemous, to
say so, but it is in Las Vegas that one comes
nearest to seeing gross matter transformed into
aetherial substance by the power of light.

Now the Eiffel Tower achieved its own kind of
aetherial quality by genius, by historical
accident – and chiefly because no one looked to
it to deliver the comforts of indoor space, and as
a result it may have accidentally set Modern
Architecture an impossible and deceiving task.
For in habitable buildings offering indoor
comforts, such effects can only be attained with

the use of power, and only when this fact is fully
understood and enthusiastically acknowledged
will there be habitable space that can rival
Gustave Eiffel's old masterwork in Paris.

There are a few promising examples around –
Philip Johnson's Glass House in New Canaan
comes nearer to it than does Mies van der
Rohe's Farnsworth House, and only a night
view can show why. But they really are few,
and it may yet prove to be a tragic flaw in
Modern Architecture that its great pioneers like
Paxton and Eiffel set up for it an aesthetic aim
whose physical implications were too vast for
even its greatest masters to encompass,
confident and competent, ambitious and
efficient as they might be. It could be that the
true and ultimate architecture of modern
space will never stand upon this Earth because
we have neither the psychological thrust nor
physical power to achieve it.

PRACTICE

Modern Architecture is not a neat chain of causes and effects, nor is it a simple strip cartoon that proceeds tidily from frame to frame. The trouble is the buildings . . . they stand about from decade to decade, obscuring the historical view and obstructing sweeping generalisations; they can take so long to design, finance and build that a couple of short-lived 'Isms' may have come and gone before the clients can move in. That is one of the reasons that the works described on the pages which now follow are arranged in only the most cursorily chronological order; I have begun with more or less the first and finished with near enough the last, but the route between is my own, not Father Time's.

Another reason for the non-systematic arrangement, over and above their sheer longevity, is that they were not built to illustrate themes or prove points. It is, unfortunately, much easier to illustrate first principles by second-rate buildings, where some gimmick-stricken architect went bald-headed to prove his mastery of concrete cantilevers or interpenetrating spaces or even modernity. The masterworks of architects both great and small may be simple, but never simple-minded; their complexities and contraditions (as Robert Venturi called them) make them perpetually rewarding and perennially unclassifiable. To force them into thematic categories, to group them under headings like those – Space, Function, and so forth – of the preceding chapters, would be to deny their nature as buildings. With one peculiar exception, each is an unique assembly of materials at a particular spot on the Earth's surface and nowhere else, conceived by and for an unrepeatable grouping of architect, builder, client. Even where a building is now valued for some particular aspect above all others, we have to face the fact that it may only stand out because it is the final and masterly flourish to a long and complex design process, deeply pondered and resolved in all its aspects. And the one valued aspect may only be so prized

because Modern Architecture's camp-followers are such a pushy and impatient lot. Throughout its history, the Modern Movement has seen its works described, criticized, pigeon-holed and footnoted, almost before completion, by pundits eager to prove their own vast knowledge by getting the key concepts down in print before the architects could frustrate them by revealing their own true, untidy and all too human motives. It is time to let the buildings stand up for themselves.

But not in isolation. They cannot, anyhow, because the buildings that exist are the mental context in which architects design the buildings that are to come. So the apparently random order of what follows does not mean that the buildings are disconnected, either in their architects' minds, my mind, nor – I suspect – will they long remain un-connected in the reader's mind. There remains one further connection to establish; the direct and obvious one between the reader and the physical presence of the buildings themselves. The descriptions that follow will succeed only if they drive the reader out to look at these works in the original.

FLATS ON THE ZAANSTRAAT AMSTERDAM

Michel de Klerk

Michel de Klerk has nothing to do with the characteristic architectural developments of our century, except that he worked in it, was inspired by at least two of the architects (Berlage and Wright) who inspired many highly characteristic twentieth-century architects, and – like those architects – he worked in the field of public housing and on the scale of the modern city. In spite of an early death in 1923, he never became a posthumous legend, and, until quite recently his name and reputation were kept alive only by oddballs like Bruno Taut.

Yet to encounter his masterpiece, the great triangular block of flats in the angle of the Zaanstraat in Amsterdam, is to be whacked on the head by one of the most violent architectural experiences this century has produced. It is truly an *'architecture autre'*, the missing complement of the modern architecture that in fact happened, but might have turned out like this, instead, but for one or two minute shifts of opinion in Europe around 1910. The assurance with which de Klerk encompasses the changing functions and considerable size of this large island site (of which only one small part is not from his designs) bespeaks a born architect and a master organiser. The management of the western end, the base of the triangle, baroque in concept but sharpened with an art-nouveau wit, is almost inconceivable in the same generation as J. J. P. Oud, with his straight rows of primly square buildings; except that Amsterdam was, for about five years, full of architects who, under de Klerk's leadership, differed from him only in not possessing his touch of genius. His chosen materials were brick, wood, tile-hanging – everything that Oud professed to hate – handled with a loving, craftsmanly care that de Klerk, quite as much as Oud, derived from Berlage. The more alien de Klerk looks to the Modern Movement, the closer he, in fact, stands to it: the long 'zeppelin' windows near the point are entirely post-futurist with a touch of Frank Lloyd Wright, and the post office with its round tower that occupies the point of the triangle is, *mutatis mutandis*, the right-handed brother of the left-handed facade of Mendelsohn's Schocken store in Stuttgart

Just behind the post office, inside the block, is a little triangular courtyard from which one looks down the gardens in the middle of the island towards a cottage building that serves as a sort of tenants' common room. The space of this little court is invaded by balconies, steps, porches, oriels, lamps, beams and other structural-functional elements, that carve in from all sides until one begins to feel a bit like the lady in the box through which the magician sticks swords and spears. This is space architecture as surely as anything spare, rectangular and undecorated, produced by the Bauhaus or the Russian Constructivists. This has the mood of the age, a little prematurely perhaps (but what about Mackintosh?) in everything, except that it is decorated. This is what modern architecture was going to look like until Adolf Loos, with his anathema on decoration, and the abstractionists, with their alternative vocabulary of undecorated forms, gave it two minute deflections from its original orbit, and ultimately set it rotating about other suns. Viewing the Zaanstraat with eyes from which all prejudice has been shocked away, one realises what a near thing it must have been.

Michel de Klerk: *Zaanstraat housing, Amsterdam, 1917, the post-office*
Zaanstraat Housing, interior courtyard

Michel de Klerk, 1884–1923, was the last of the romantic, short-lived prodigy pioneers, an immensely inventive but literally sick talent. He and his Amsterdam contemporaries, like Piet Kramer, pushed the structural implications of Art Nouveau beyond even the point where they had been abandoned by Mackintosh.

SCHRÖDER HOUSE UTRECHT

Gerrit T. Rietveld

A cardboard Mondriaan: so it was once called, more in perplexity than derision. It is one of two works of world consequences by Rietveld – the other is his famous 'red-blue' chair – and yet, when one looks at it, there could hardly be a less likely candidate for fame. Tiny, structurally timid, badly sited, undistinguished in plan, it may once have had compelling local and private virtues for its inhabitants that are now difficult to make convincing to outsiders, but what assures it its place in the world scene is its exterior. Here for the first time, in 1924, the aesthetic possibilities of the hard school of modern architecture were uncompromisingly and brilliantly revealed (no early house of Le Corbusier is comparable until 1926, his first vintage year). The small cube of the house expands in a proliferation of flyaway planes, horizontal and vertical, that sometimes collide in right-angled intersections. There may be a long-range debt to Wright, but the implications of Wright's domestic space-games have been purged and made clean through the aesthetic detergency of European abstract art. The surfaces are, indeed, as smooth and as neutral as those of a Mondriaan painting, in similar colours, relieved only by a use of glass that emphasises its immaterial quality (unlike the jewelled presence of the glass in Wright's Robie House) and by a few lean, sparse metal stanchions that support the edges of some of the flying planes, and steam-pipe hand-rails that make some of the planes usable as balconies. Machine aesthetic; rectangular space play; the bare minimum of the modern architecture that was to be.

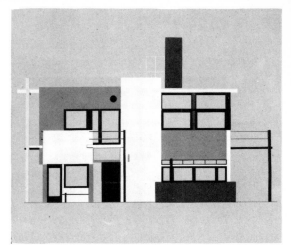

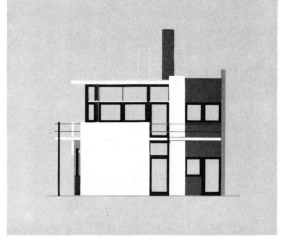

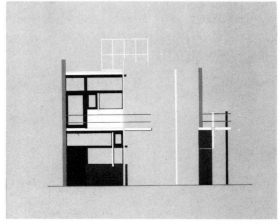

G. T. Rietveld: *Schröder house, Utrecht, 1924*

G. T. Rietveld, born in 1888, has been mentioned already for his other significant contribution to modern design, the 'red/blue' chair (p. 29). No-one, not even his official biographer, Theodore M. Brown, has yet been able to suggest why this very competent, but otherwise unremarkable provincial figure should *twice* have contributed such symptomatic objects to the rise of the Modern Movement, and at his death in 1964 he still remained an enigmatic but revered figure.

FLATS IN ST JAMES'S PLACE LONDON

Denys Lasdun

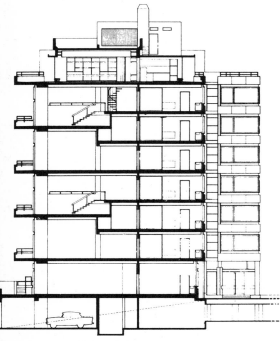

St James's Place flats, section showing one-and-a-half-storey living-rooms

Denys Lasdun: *flats in St James's Place, London, 1961*

Eric Lyons: *SPAN housing, Ham Common, 1956*

James's, overlooking Green Park.

A luxury building is still not an easy assignment for an English architect to undertake (maybe this is an aspect of the conscience of the architectural profession that should be nurtured for the common good) since modern architecture here has grown up so closely with progressive politics that non-proletarian housing is still something of a moral embarrassment to us. It's easier, in some ways, for us to build, and criticise, Stirling and Gowan's picturesque, atmospheric and studiedly graceless exercise in working-class re-housing at Preston, than Eric Lyon's relaxed, eye-soothing – but middle-class – housing for the various SPAN developments around London. But it may be that the middle is the real problem, not the ends of the social spectrum, for Denys Lasdun has worked with complete conviction at both extremes: his cluster-block slum-clearance housing in Bethnal Green, and his almost overpoweringly luxurious block of skip-level flats down a turning off St.

Lasdun's success in St. James is basically that he has created luxury in terms of unmistakably modern architecture, and by the architectural means that are peculiar to the Modern Movement. Not fringed drapes and ankle-deep carpets but the basic luxuries of expansive spaces and lavish environmental services. By post-war British standards the spaces are enormous, and in the one-and-a-half storey living rooms one swims, adrift in sheer volume. On the services side, the heating is conspicuously adequate, the kitchens mechanised to the eyebrows and, above all, the sound insulation is of TV-studio quality. It is London's most comprehensive demonstration of what modern architecture has to offer in the sense of a controlled and euphoric environment, physically and aesthetically satisfying before any stick of furniture or work of art has been installed.

Best of all, Lasdun has made the emphasis on space and services the source of expression on the exterior. The skip-level section, with its one-and-a-half storey units introducing a contrapuntal rhythm in the stacking of the floors, gives him almost sufficient subtleties of proportion and pattern to be able to do without any further architecture on the exterior: all that is to be seen are the edges of the balconies (which become the spandrels where the windows are up flush with the facade) establishing the main horizontals, and the ducts for the services, establishing the main verticals. Such extravagant simplicity needs to be almost offensively well detailed – and is. The vertical ducts are built of a rich dark brick as used in engineering, and the balcony fronts have aprons of choice marbles (pieces were sent back, if not choice enough). The windows are carried in bronze frames of conspicuously *de luxe* specification, and the exposed concrete work of the pent-house structure has been so skilfully poured, into shutterings so carefully built, out of what appears to be planks specially selected for their grain patterns, that shaggy old Brutalist shutter-patterned concrete is transmuted into an exquisite fine-art material.

Denys Lasdun: *Cluster-block, London, 1958*

Denys Lasdun, born 1914, does not fit comfortably into the generation-bound structure of the Modern Movement in England, his career beginning *just* before World War Two. Nor does his output fit into tidy categories either – originally seen as a brilliant stylist in the field of mass-housing and the inventor of new forms for social architecture (see p 72) he now seems established as the creator of 'representational' buildings like the Royal College of Surgeons and the new National Theatre in London.

St James's Place flats,
street
elevation

73

FACTORY AT BRYN MAWR WALES

Architects' Co-Partnership

FACTORY AT BLUMBERG GERMANY

Egon Eiermann

FACTORY AT MERLO ARGENTINA

Marco Zanuso

Bryn Mawr was designed by ACP – **Architects Co-Partnership** – one of a number of post-war attempts to found egalitarian organisat·ons (cf TAC, The Architects' Collaborative, in the US) without any figurehead to act as the focus for an architectural cult of personality. **Albert Kahn**'s office contributed an immense quantity of sound, clean, businesslike and sometimes inspired factory buildings to the US automobile industry in the twenties and thirties, and became an exemplar for enlightened industrialists all over the world. **Sir Owen Williams's** factory for Messrs Boots at Beeston, Notts, was succeeded by a series of other exemplary structures, such as the Peckham Health Centre, that helped to build him an impressive reputation – later somewhat diminished by his rather unimpressive work on the M1 motorway.

For a movement officially committed to industrialisation, modern architecture has contributed awfully little to the pregress of the modern factory. Most of the best or most celebrated examples have been the work of engineering offices like Albert Kahn's in the US, or Sir Owen Williams' in Britain. It cannot be that there is no distinctive contribution that an architect can make, but often the architect's contribution seems distinctive in the dubious sense as well as the good. In the well-known rubber factory at Bryn Mawr – one of the first major pieces of post-war British architecture – the mark of the architect is seen as much in the dated conception of the fashiony, undulating roofs of the ancillary structures as in the grand, and still convincing, central conception of nine clustered domes covering the main work-spaces – one of the most impressive interiors in Britain since St. Paul's.

But the darling of post-war architect-designed factories, and rightly so since it seems to resist the corrosions of time and fickle fashion better than any other, is the little textile plant at Blumberg in the Black Forest, designed by Egon Eiermann (who also did the German Pavilion at the Brussels Exhibition of 1958).

Blumberg's basic attraction lies in having all the modest attributes of industrial architecture to an almost immodest degree; the immodesty lying in the acute visual skill with which they are handled. The main weaving shed has a steel frame and corrugated asbestos cladding; so have thousands of other factories, but they don't have Blumberg's carefully worked out system of external framing and uninterrupted bands of cladding – ponder this building carefully and you will begin to see the difference between mere utilitarian construction and inspired functional architecture. Equally, the boiler-house is an exercise in the machine aesthetic, so beautifully detailed and proportioned that it is almost in the Mies van der Rohe class – though, inevitably, there isn't the spare money on an industrial commission to support the ultimate refinements that Mies normally demands of a design. Even so, Blumberg comes as close as

dammit to that ideal of eloquent reticence that so many functionalists saw as the aim of modern architecture: is this to be attributed in any way to the fact that Eiermann cut his teeth, in design, on stage sets?

Factories may indeed be theatrical – industry provides images of drama that have long fired the minds of modern architects – but even more important, probably, is the fact that industry still lies outside the magic confines of 'culture' and certain rules of decorum and restraint aren't felt to apply. Experiments can be made that might not in serious architecture.
So, after almost a decade of theorising about changeable buildings with clip-on components, during which time none of any consequence got built in fields like housing, schools and other normal subject matter for architecture, one at least got built in the field of factory building. It's an interesting design on any account, this local branch factory for Olivetti typewriters at Merlo in Argentina, designed by the Milanese architect Marco Zanuso.

The structure, for a start, consists of deep concrete tubes carried on long rows of divided columns. From the sides of each of these parallel tubes grow a pair of flat concrete shelves, and vertical members rising from the shelves carry the edges of roof slabs that span from the shelf of one tube to that of the next – and the vertical gap from shelf to roof can be glazed, where appropriate, to give good industrial lighting while keeping the weather out. Put a wall round the outside and you have the basic shelter. Then plug-in or clip-on air-conditioner units at the open end of all appropriate tubes and allow the conditioned air to blow out through slots in the underside of the tube and you have something a lot more habitable than mere basic shelter.
And since the air-conditioners will certainly wear out or become obsolescent long before the structure, they can be un-plugged and replaced. This happens in all other air-conditioned buildings, of course, but none of the others have the wit or imagination to make a visible architectural virtue of the fact.

Architects' Co-Partnership: *Factory, Bryn Mawr, 1953*

Egon Eiermann: *factory, Blumberg, 1951*

Marco Zanuso: *factory, Merlo 1964*

EAMES HOUSE
PACIFIC
PALISADES
CALIFORNIA
Charles Eames

FORD HOUSE
AURORA
ILLINOIS
Bruce Goff

Charles Eames: *Eames House, Santa Monica, 1949*

76

Frank Lloyd Wright's claim to be the ultimate all-American architect is a strong one, and he was not averse to making it himself. Yet it is a claim that relates to a rather special view of America; large, un-specific, Olympian, rhetorical, like the poetry of Walt Whitman. He remained always something of *Grand-Maitre* in the European tradition (beret, cloak and all) rather than the Mr. Fixit of the nitty-gritty, not to say grass-roots, tradition of the Americans who 'got learned mechanicking down on the farm'.

There are two other equally individualistic architects who, in their very different ways, seem to pick up these down-home, do-it-yourself aspects of America better than most others – Charles Eames and Bruce Goff. Both have a sort of hot-rodder attitude to the elements of building, ingeniously mating off-the-peg components, specials, and off-cuts from other technologies. Eames's own house, almost the only building for which he is known, is largely made of standard industrial components and structural members intended for a different version of the design on another part of the site. Yet you'd never know it; the finished building is of such studied composure and fine-drawn elegance that it can still put many later examples of this persuasion to shame Persuasion is the right word; the Eames house was one of the most persuasive of its generation, it taught the whole world a way of seeing. Not on its own, but as part of a total and complete Eames vision, that was timely (much of the Festival of Britain in 1951 had a similar air) and totally right in style. The quality of the Eames vision is closely linked to the sudden availability of more and cheaper colour photography and colour printing and colour movies in the post-war years. We were dazzled and seduced by a vision of abundant and glowing colour, but also by the objects that vision presented to us. The world perceived by the eye and lens of Eames, his wife Ray, and a brilliant generation of assistants and collaborators, was discovered to be full of extraordinary objects of art, craft, industry, past, present, West, East, primitive and sophisticated, common or rare, which no one

Eames house, standard factory windows and exterior views

Charles Eames, born 1907, is reportedly very tired of being called a Renaissance Man, but it is still hard to find a term more apt for this all-rounder whose apparently unstoppable inventiveness has given us a series of classic chairs from 1946 onwards, films on every topic (it seems) from communication theory to spinning tops since 1953, brilliant toys (especially the Deck of Cards) and exhibitions that range from the principles of mathematics to the life of Pandit Nehru – not forgetting key innovations in audio-visual education, and that house which is still regarded by many as one of the touchstones of recent architecture.

Bruce Goff: *Ford house,*
Aurora, Illinois, 1950

seemed to have noticed before. Re-seen by the Eames persuasion, they proved to be almost works of art – perhaps because the Eameses themselves were prepared to treat them as art, collecting them, displaying them, filling the house with them until it became a treasure chest of new-found beauties. It also became, in the process, part of the world's vision, known, admired and visited from all parts of the globe where art and design are practised. If you are looking for a more purely American vision; one that belongs like beer belongs, looks at home in Marlboro' country, and is as simultaneously familiar and astonishing as a Howard Johnson, it's more likely to be the architecture of Bruce Goff. For him the European mind seeks desperate similes: in his ability to mould the off-cuts of standardised America nearer to heart's desire, he is an even more radical hot-rodder than Eames; he digs exotic cultures, far-out musics, a-formal arts, so that it is difficult nowadays not to see him as some sort of hipster: consumer-oriented, sensitive to grass-roots public moods, he is the master of the dream-house; without formal academic training, he has devoted much of his life to a Socratic teaching relationship with the young; and though he was once Wright's most fervid admirer and remains a devotee of the immortal memory, there has been no real sign of Wright in his works since the late thirties.

What he has developed since then defies categorisation, and since there is no stylistic consistency running through it, there is no

Bruce Goff, born in 1904, has existed too long on the margins of fame, designing houses of unclassifiable originality in the Middle West, and suffering periodical discoveries by pundits with axes to grind. He deserves the opportunity to do a big building on a conspicuous site, and thus silence both his critics and his admirers.

building to point out as typical. The Ford house at Aurora, Illinois, is my personal favourite because I relish the wit with which elements of other structures and other technologies have been re-deployed. The basic bulk of the house is, in form, a sort of squashed-doughnut dome, which has no visible relationship with anyone else's domes, and is built over reclaimed Quonsett (Nissen) hut frames (the army surplus aesthetic!). Some of this framing is skinned over with wood or glass, but some is not, making a kind of close garden occupying a segment equal to almost a quarter of the domed space, and for a large part of the circle, the Quonsett frames are grounded on a dwarf wall of blocks of straight-run channel coal. Flanking quarter domes provide bedroom space, the main dome sheltering a giant living and working room, with a saucer-shaped floor cantilevered out from the central chimney to provide something between a sanctum sanctorum and a tree-house.

All up, the house has the mad logic of so much that happens in the Middle West, and the same irrefutable justifications by local standards. One of the freedoms that Americans don't enjoy as often as they might is the freedom to live in a house designed as if houses had just been invented, but this isn't for want of trying on Goff's part.

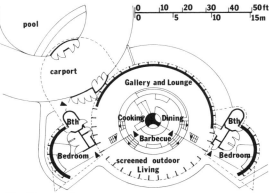

Ford house, plan

PENGUIN POOL LONDON ZOO
Lubetkin and Tecton

Not many modern buildings achieve instant
popular success, but the Penguin Pool at the
London Zoo outstandingly did; and for
something like fifteen years it held a unique
place as the only playful piece of modern
architecture in Britain, until the Festival of
1951. The high popular regard was in some ways
unfair to the numerous other first class zoo
buildings designed by the Tecton partnership
that centred on Berthold Lubetkin for most of
the thirties, forties and fifties, yet the esteem is
not undeserved. For a long time this oval hole
in the ground with its interlocking spiral ramps
was out-and-away the least inhibited and least
parochial new building in Britain, and it could
probably stand examination in its own right as
a piece of abstract sculpture of the Anglo-
constructivist epoch (the period when Naum
Gabo was still working in England). It can also
stand up as a pretty crisp piece of concrete
engineering for its period; those ramps, though
small, must impose some curious twisting loads
on their points of anchorage, and are reputed to
be practically solid steel reinforcing with a thin
cover of concrete. But chiefly, and permanently,
the Penguin Pool stands up by reason of its
entire aptness to its subject matter and purpose.
To the best possible advantage it exhibits the
pompous-ridiculous antics of the penguins to
the human race whose pompous-ridiculous
behaviour the penguins unwittingly ape. In
honour of their unconscious mockery, the
penguins were flattered with a rather better
building than was available to most English
human beings of the period. There must be some
moral in this.

*Penguin Pool, showing
spiral ramps*

Berthold Lubetkin's
involvement with modern
architecture goes back to the
Revolutionary years in Russia
(where he was born in 1901)
and in the late twenties he
was one of those strolling
Soviet talents, like Ehrenburg
or Mayakowsky. He settled
in England in 1930. The Tecton
partnership, which lasted in

one form or another until
almost the end of the fifties,
served as the training ground
for a large proportion of two
successive generations of
British modernists.

TOWN HALL KURASHIKI JAPAN

KOFU COMMUNI-CATIONS CENTRE

Kenzo Tange

The small poetic figure of **Kenzo Tange**, born 1913, has become increasingly familiar around the world as his growing fame causes him to be invited hither and yon. His output is not very large; its power lies in its ability to combine a convincing primitivism with an almost Futurist view of city planning which, however, has mostly been expressed in unexecuted projects so far.

One of the most heartening proofs of the continuing vitality of modern architecture is the way Japanese architects have not gone the expected way. Western pundits, critics and informed circles generally had the forward path for Japanese architecture mapped out as a confluence of the native *Sukiya* tradition (informal, black-and-white in the manner of the Katsura Palace) and the Mondriaan wing of European abstract art; the outcome was expected to be something like Mies van der Rohe, and they had even picked the architect who was going to do it; Junzo Sakakura, designer of the sweet and elegant Japanese pavilion at the Paris exhibition of 1937.

It is with real relief that one reports that everybody was wrong, and that Sakakura's fine-drawn early architecture has been trampled underfoot in the stampede to create the real Japanese modern architecture, under the undoubted leadership of Kenzo Tange, who established himself in half-a-dozen years as one of the world's outstanding architects. Tange's architecture, most eloquently summed up in the Town Hall he designed for Kurashiki, under the enlightened patronage of the Ohara clan, is an architecture of enormous mass, fortress-like solidity, aggressively three-dimensional plasticity. Where the West had expected steel to be used as the equivalent of the slender wooden posts of the *Sukiya* tradition, Tange uses concrete beams as the equivalents of the tree-trunk columns and thundering wooden bracketting of Japanese monumental architecture. The town hall stands on a ponderous concrete chassis raised on substantial, no-nonsense columns that batter (i.e. taper) inwards towards the top, like the lower walls of some *shogun* fortress. The longer side-beams of this chassis erupt at the ends in two sub-beams, like the ends of some planking system, and the same sort of device, but protruding in both directions and interlocking, happens at the corners of the roof slab. In between, the main walls are apparently built up of horizontal concrete planks (some of them omitted to make windows) which collide and interlock at the corners of the block in a manner that says 'log-cabin' in any language.

The originality of all this is so striking and so exciting that it is difficult to believe that Tange has arrived at it in a matter of five years from his prim, square, Mieso-Corbusian city hall for Tokyo.

Whatever Mies had to contribute to Tange's style is buried and forgotten now, but the Corbusian inspiration shows through even at Kurashiki. The council chamber has been fairly described as Ronchamp-inside-out, or a floating cocoon within the structure of the building. The slope of the ceiling becomes the rake of the ramped seating of a complementary outdoor auditorium on the roof, and this contributes an irregular diagonal element to the silhouette, in contrast to the square block below, much as Le Corbusier often uses roof-top irregularities to set off the standard grids of his facades.

But the entrance hall reveals a positively meta-Corbusian style. The stairwell is dark, overscale. The stair ascends in straight flights, left-handed with a half-landing, cantilevered out from walls that are roughly shutter-patterned exposed concrete, relieved – if that is the word – by window openings that are like nothing so much as mediaeval firing-slits. The effects have been called Piranesian, which is justifiable as long as the term is only applied to the lighting, the spatial play. But there is nothing of Piranesi or his inflated classicism about any element that one could actually touch with the hand. These, as we now begin to see, are the inevitable result of a union of French rationalist thinking about concrete as a manner of building in post and beams (Tange clearly knows his Corbusier), and a Japanese manner of thinking of architecture as the massive combination of heroically scaled horizontals and uprights. The result transcends both, and gives an architecture whose reciprocal effect on the West may be sensational. For, with the appearance of Tange, Japanese architecture ceases to be a colonial export from Europe, and becomes an independent national style in its own very emphatic right. What is more, Tange himself becomes a figure of world influence, particularly after the world had seen his two

Kenzo Tange: *Town Hall,*
Kurashiki, 1960, main
staircase

83

Town Hall, Kurashiki

Kofu communications centre, concrete structure

swimming pools for the Tokyo Olympics in 1964. His reputation could give strength to those with whom he was associated – when Japan's revolutionary 'Metabolist' group of visionary architects burst upon the scene in those same years, their projects for giant urban megastructures gained credibility from the fact that Tange was also doing megastructures in the same vein.

Designing them, that is. Other architects in other countries were to build the few megastructures that exist, but Tange's huge project for a whole new suburb of Tokyo strung out on suspension bridges across the Bay remains the classic of the *genre*. The nearest he has ever come to a building that catches the eloquently provisional relationship between circulation and habitation that informs most megastructure projects – the circulation-ways remain fixed, the habitable spaces come and go at need – is the Kofu Communications Centre.

The circulation there is vertical; four square groups, each of four lift/stair/service towers, so arranged as to give a file of paired towers down the centre, some of the pairs being joined near the top. Not all the towers reach this height however, one is four storeys shorter, others achieve intermediate heights, deliberately giving the impression that they are 'high enough for now' but could be raised later if more storeys of accommodation were added.

Equally deliberately, the accommodation has the air of having been hooked in, box by box, between the towers, the visible chassis under each box being connected to the supporting towers by massive brackets that resemble, on an heroic scale, the cast-iron joiners of an old-fashioned bed-frame. It is only when you stop and ponder the true nature of all that beautifully finished concrete, that it becomes clear that this cannot be the way the Centre is assembled; the almighty arms of power that could lift out and re-arrange these 25-metre boxes of habitable spaces have not been made, nor ever will be. What Tange offers is, so to speak, a metaphor of adaptability. But what a resounding metaphor!

Communications centre, Kofu,
1967

85

LABORATORIES IN PHILADELPHIA

Louis Kahn

Richards Laboratories. Philadelphia, 1960

It is not subtlety or musicianship that makes a popular song, but a good gimmick or punch-line in every verse. So, too, with a building that becomes the rage of the hour – whatever professional craft and architectural skill Louis Kahn may have invested in every part of the Richards Medical Laboratories in Philadelphia, its uncontrollable success depends on just two simple and superficial things: its picturesque silhouette of clustered towers, and the fact that those towers are mostly for services. It is not easy to say which of these is the more important consideration, because they appear to have run as closely together in Kahn's mind as in that of his admiring public.

Taken in bulk, this busy assemblage of expressively articulated vertical masses and comparatively fragile looking horizontal truss-work, complex and irregular in plan, is a reaction against the smooth anonymity of the Mies tradition, that would have wrapped up the whole project in one exquisite crystalline box, and this reaction clearly chimed in with the increasingly picturesque mood of the post-Brutalist world (Kahn is one of the Brutalists' favourite architects). But, in addition, this is a building whose functions demand a formidable array of mechanical services (to clear off toxic atmospheres from the laboratories) and Kahn has expressed this with an equally formidable array of brick monoliths crowding closely about the glass boxes with the laboratories in them. Nothing could make more clear or more dramatic Kahn's concept of the servant spaces (towers) and the served spaces (laboratories), and to a profession increasingly concerned with the problem of packing mechanical services – bigger and more complex every year – into or around their designs, the Philadelphia towers were triumphant proof that the solution of the services problem could be monumental architecture. One point remained to be resolved however: was it architecturally honest to make something so very monumental ('Duct-henge' was the ribald estimate) out of anything so transient and changeable as services, here today and obsolete tomorrow? Might not Zanuso's clip-on solution at Merlo be more honest while no less eloquent?

Louis Kahn, Estonian born in 1901, and the great luminary of the 'Philadelphia School' of architects, was a late-emerging talent, unappreciated until the decline of dogmatic Functionalism set younger architects in search of traditional values in architecture. He first attained world notice with his Yale art gallery of 1955, became the object of a fanatical cult of personality, which had settled into a sincere and devoted admiration by two full generations of students and followers by the time of his death in 1974.

US ATOMIC
ENERGY
COMMISSION
PAVILION
1960
Victor Lundy and
Walter Bird

Victor Lundy: *US Atomic
Energy Commission Pavilion,
1959*

Like a friendly whale, or something equally
organic, the US Atomic Energy Commission's
portable exhibition/theatre toured the world for
almost a decade before people began to
understand that they had seen a pioneering
masterpiece float by. Inflated structures of all
sorts were to become a student craze and an
essential part of Pop festivals in the late Sixties,
but by that time the USAEC double-dome had
been around so long that historians had to
re-discover it for the world.

Designed in 1960 by an architect better known
for wooden structures in Florida, and Walter
Bird, the true founder of usable pneumatic
architecture, the theatre was, in effect, an
enormous balloon with a double skin, and the
earth's surface forming its underside. The
double skin with pressurised air between the
skins gave protection against puncturing and
collapse, but all this exterior was, in its turn
supported by air-pressure within the exhibition
space itself. None of these pressures were very
high, not enough to notice even, and low enough
to be kept in by conventional revolving doors
at the entrances and exists. It travelled the
world with its own compressors and auxiliaries,
took about a day to erect – which was longer
than a circus big-top but vastly qaicker than
most portable exhibition structures.

All in all, with its double-breasted profile and
gaping mouth it gave a more weird and
wonderful preview of the technical future than
any of the Atoms-for-Peace propaganda inside
it. But because it was an American exhibit there
was always the risk of politically-inspired
sabotage – hence the complication of the double
skin. Such precautions were rarely needed for
the smaller inflatables of the next generation,
since they were themselves the work of
precisely the sort of activists who would object
to Yankee Imperialism and the Vietnam War.
In every conceivable shape from the geometric
to the phallic and in every opaque or
transparent colour that modern plastics
technology can afford, they were unbelievably
quick and easy to build – any commune that
contained a couple of girls who could cut paper
dress-patterns, any transcendental family with

USAEC pavilion, entrance
Victor Lundy and **Birdair
Structures** are at first sight
an odd pair of collaborators –
Lundy, born 1921, a pupil of
Gropius in the sternest years
of his headship of the Harvard
Design School; Birdair,
pioneer manufacturers of
inflatables, founded in 1956
by Walter Bird, the man who
ten years earlier had got
inflatables into a practicable
condition for the first time
while working on lightweight
shelters for arctic radar at
Princeton University.
But Lundy had always been
one of the more unpredictably
brilliant Gropians, breaking
early from the rectangular
geometry of the International
style to design elegant, even
decorative, arched wooden
structures for functions
ranging from churches to
shoe stores.

*The author
televising from
Tony Gwilliam's
Do-it-yourself
inflatable*

access to a stapler or a plastic-welder could
contrive a sizable inflatable in a couple of days,
sometimes much less. Students with no visible
knowledge of aerodynamics cut compressor fans
from biscuit-tin lids and powered them with
army-surplus electric motors; inflatable
structures bubbled up on the lawns of
universities, the front steps of architectural
schools and adorned almost every manifestation
of the Alternative Culture.

They are now being taken up more and more by
serious minded commercial users and
government officials are devising regulations to
bring them within the rule of law, but
inflatables will never quite recover from the
image of gaiety and improvisation with which
the late Sixties endowed them, nor from their
ancestry in a great white Moby-distention that
set out to tell the people something portentous
about atomics, but showed them instead the
vision of a living breathing architecture they
had never known before.

89

Giuseppe Terragni:
Novocomum Block, Como,
1927

Como and the Italian lakes have a reputation for producing masons and architects. They contributed major talents to the middle ages and the early Baroque, and another gaggle of Comacines produced Italy's most serious contribution to the first phase of modern architecture. Antonio Sant'Elia, one of the bright stars of the Futurist epoch, was born in Como but built no buildings there, but his drawings, his example, his legend were the inspiration of the Italian 'rationalist' architecture of the twenties and thirties. Though he anathematised monuments and monumentality, his name appears on a gigantic monument on the shores of Lake Como that is unmistakably Santelian in style. It was worked up, from a number of his sketches for other things, by Enrico Prampolini and Giuseppe Terragni, whose career and death in the Second World War were an almost exact repeat of Sant'Elia's a generation earlier, except that Terragni built buildings, nearly all of them in Como.

They are a remarkable group; the education of an architect in five structures. First the Monument to Sant'Elia and the dead of the First World War, a stark, symmetrical composition of abstract forms, a white dipylon braced by canted buttresses rising from a base of grey stone – not yet modern, but a drastically purged classicism. Then *Novocomum*, the block of flats behind the Fascist stadium. It preserves the symmetry, but everything else is harsh and deliberate modernism borrowed from Berlin and Bolshevik Moscow. Nothing could be more period and dated than the edgy alternation of bull-nosed and sharp-arrised corners that contribute most of the visible 'architecture' on the exterior. Then comes maturity with a rush: the Casa del Fascio, one of the most brilliant formal exercises of the thirties. Functionally, it simply stacks floors of offices around the side of an internal court, the front opening up into an exposed structural frame. The interior is no more nor less offensive than other Italian interiors of the period; it has the air of being made of materials at once pretentiously shoddy and incredibly permanent, but the front, seen across the piazza outside the cathedral and theatre, is stunning –

Giuseppe Terragni (with Enrico Prampolini): *Monument, Como, 1926*

Terragni was born in 1904, and died in 1943 after experiences on the Russian front which permanently damaged his mind. While the quality of his work makes him a figure of undoubted world standing, his equivocal relationship to the Mussolini regime also makes him a figure of controversy – one can safely say, however, that his was a great talent ruined by Fascism.

a monumental diagram of the rules of *divina proporzione* immortalised in marble. For those who believe that modern architecture is still subject to the grand old rules, it is proof that the rules are still valid. For those who believe that modern architecture has to do with social progress, it is the machine aesthetic at its most heartlessly elegant. But, outside the official Fascist context, Terragni is not heartless. The Casa Giuliani-Frigerio, nearer the lake again, is a blithely fashionable exercise in the style of Rietveld's Schröder House, with external flyaway sun-screens and balcony frames. It is the father of several thousand cut-price variants in post-war Italian Suburbs, but its freshness is quite untarnished by its nasty progeny. The fifth and most humane of his significant buildings in Como, is an infant school, the Asilo Sant'Elia, the most fairy-godfatherly compliment ever paid to the young by a modern architect. Here, Terragni's passion for open frames and courtyard plans produces a delicate environment of airy, lightly-shaded spaces and framed views of greenery beyond, unaffected (though not without its formalisms) and still, to my mind, the best school built in Italy in this century.

CASA DEL GIRASOLE ROME
Luigi Moretti

HOUSE ON THE ZATTERE VENICE
Ignazio Gardella

Some buildings are embarrassingly modern: they become tests of taste, like the Casa del Girasole, which was much argued over in the early fifties. Its architect, though a man of formidable culture and intellect, was not quite trusted in some architectural circles, and his doubtful position, as expressed in his work, enables him to throw revealing light into skeleton-haunted cupboards. Long before the eruption of Neoliberty (the Art Nouveau revival) called the progressive aims of modern Italian architecture into question, the Girasole had made them look pretty dubious. What goes on inside it is in no way modern; routine Roman

apartments, planned along a corridor, and composed into a block raised above the street by a basement full of servants and services, as in all Italy back to the Quattrocento. But the exterior is unmistakably modern, *Italian* modern, like the most serious work of his Milanese contemporaries. Standing wide over its narrow basement, it is as modern as the *Pavillon Suisse* standing wide over its pilotis.

If this were just window-dressing, a veneer of modernity, the Girasole could be dismissed and conscience salved. But its modernity is not just skin-deep. Moretti has cogently argued that the

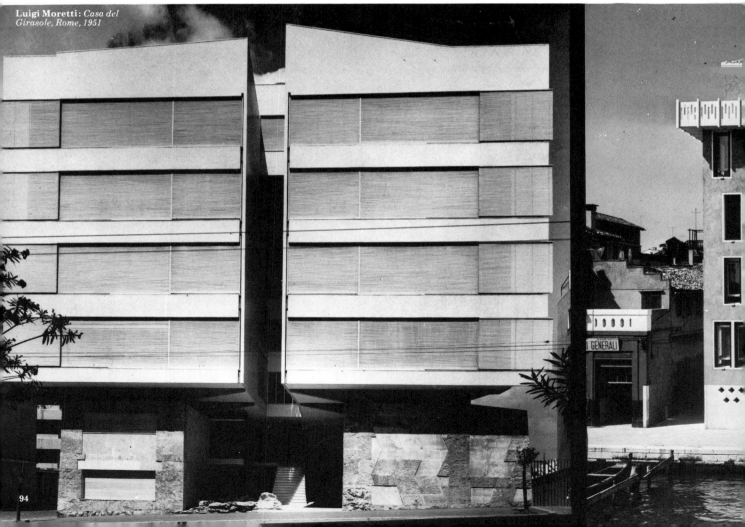

Luigi Moretti: *Casa del Girasole, Rome, 1951*

split of the facade follows inexorably from the divided plan, and having thus made modern-type architecture out of bourgeois degenerate planning, he rubs in the message with wit. The facade is made to look like a false front, yet the apparently useless extensions of the walls beyond the limits of the rooms are to provide roll-away space for the shutters, and although the concrete frame of the building is nowhere exposed, Moretti strip-teases the limbs of classical statuary among the rustication of the lower walls, as if secret caryatids were holding it all up. 'A joke', we all said, 'all right as long as it doesn't go any further' and Moretti did not pursue it. Yet something very like it was done, for quite different ends, in Venice by Ignazio Gardella. His apartment house on the Zattere degli Incurabili is an extraordinarily witty capriccio of modern and vernacular themes that add up to a new building which looks so much like a conversion job that it vanishes into the Venetian townscape the moment your attention wanders. It is fancy-dress architecture, certainly, but the very manner of its disappearance is proof that the dressing-up has not been done for the usual reasons of historical cowardice. Very tricky . . .

Ignazio Gardella: *house on the Zattere, Venice, 1957*

Wright's own estimate of the nature of his Prairie Houses was set out in the introduction to the classic portfolio of drawings published in Berlin in 1910. The text, slightly modified, can be found in: *Frank Lloyd Wright on Architecture*, edited by Frederick Gutheim (1941, and later paperbacks) and in *Frank Lloyd Wright, Buildings and Writings*, edited by Edgar Kauffman (1960).

All his long life Frank Lloyd Wright remained, as the saying went, the greatest living master of the nineteenth century; his admiration of craftsmanship long outlived his mechanistic enthusiasms of around 1900, and many of his most salutary designs of the twentieth century can best be regarded as final versions of nineteenth-century themes. The Robie House is one such: its importance as a mentor to the domestic architects of the present century is beyond question, but it is hardly modern architecture in any stylistic sense. Its surface affinities are with a tradition of *de luxe* suburban villas that reaches right back into the Victorian epoch and beyond.

The Modernist admirers of the Robie House have emphasised its abstract and spatial qualities, the great oversailing roofs, east-west below, north-south above; and the massive megalith of the central chimney that binds all together and makes sense of the rather vague relationship between the expanses of roof and the plans of the rooms below them. But, at close range on the side-walk, the visitor is much more conscious of the fact that he is confronted with such familiar impedimenta of suburbia as dwarf-walls, giant flower vases, shrubs and leaded lights. This image of a familiar tarnished and sentimental dream can be so overwhelming that the house that launched the modern movement almost single-handed, tends to vanish, momentarily, behind a haze of old associations and resentments.

Yet it is through these very details that the originality of the Robie House begins to re-assert itself as one looks. The brickwork, before the mortar was mistakenly re-pointed flush with the brick surface, had horizontally raked joints (the mortar set back about half an inch from the brick face) so that whereas there was brick, there was also an obsessive horizontal interest, to which the long continuous planes of the stone cappings to the walls contribute, as also do the squat spreading forms of those exaggerated flower vases. Before you have lifted your eyes from the garden wall you are deeply involved with the themes of horizontality and overhang.

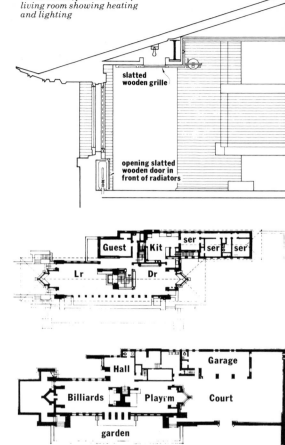

Robie House, part-section of living room showing heating and lighting

Even the diamond tracery of the leaded lights has the diamonds wider than they are high, making a sprawling, horizontal, glass-consuming, privacy-keeping, pattern of arrow-head forms that echo the arrow-head plan of the ends of the main rooms. The decoration is, indeed, everywhere congruent with the house and its functions from the smallest detail to the total effect of the bulk form, pushing out horizontally, invading and surrounding space.

The men who brushed aside its superficial suburbanities as irrelevant, in order to concentrate on its play of planes in space, knew it only from photographs – except for the man who built the only European version that

is even remotely comparable in quality. Rob van t'Hoff had worked briefly in Wright's office, knew the Robie House at first hand and drew his Dutch colleagues' attention to it. His version, the celebrated villa at Huis ter Heide, outside Utrecht, is the exact half-way house between the American inspiration and the final European realisation of a new architecture. In search of formal purity, its exterior deliberately sacrifices Wright's Arts-and-Crafts surfaces, but its interior seems almost inadvertently to fritter away in niggling complexities the magisterial expansiveness of Wright's sense of space. Perhaps it did so because van t'Hoff and all the other Europeans never divined the true source of its lurking

modernity. Behind the raked brickwork and the leaded windows the house is laced with critical technical innovations – welded steel in the roof (so much for Wright's 'Truth to Materials'!) and a heating and lighting system that is totally integrated into the structure and its decoration. European purists probably saw this as no more than a pre-occupation with 'comfort', but it was this total unity of structure and services that made the huge, easy, beautiful spaces of the Robie House possible, and it represents a degree of integration and an understanding of – above all – electric lighting that was not to be matched again for decades.

Rob van t'Hoff: *Villa, Huis ter Heide, Utrecht, 1917*

SCHOCKEN STORE STUTTGART

Eric Mendelsohn

That which the gods seek to destroy, they first frighten with near misses. The Schocken store survived the pulverisation-bombing of central Stuttgart by inches and stood up as a symbol of commercial persistence among the ruins; remained to become an object of pilgrimage for a generation re-discovering its period and its designer, Eric Mendelsohn, and – just when it was beginning to be recognised as one of the true masterpieces of the twenties – its owners and Stuttgart's megalomaniac traffic-planners had it pulled down.

Mendelsohn has never been an easy architect to assess: his practice (largely commercial while he stayed in Germany) his patrons (Jewish) his doctrine (structural expressionism) and his vocabulary of rounded and rhetorical forms, are all rather alien to the mainstream of the modern movement, even though derived from similar sources (Wright, machinery, structural technique and so forth). All this would have been no bother had Mendelsohn been a negligible architect, but he was not. He was brilliant, perhaps a sort of genius, and he gave to department-store design the same kind of radical authority as Gropius could give to institutional buildings. His Columbushaus in Berlin, or his second Schocken store in Chemnitz, may seem more immediately convincing in photographs, but to encounter the Stuttgart version in the original was to see what he had to offer. Many architects have paid lip-service to the excitement of outdoor advertising, but Mendelsohn could really do it, he had the mind for *reklame*. Schocken's non-advertising side-walls were model exercises in unobtrusive but well-architected functionalism, but the main facade on the Eberhard-Ludwigstrasse was something else again. Its ground floor was, in sheer acreage of plate glass, competitive with any of its contemporaries, but above this the brick-work of the side-walls slashed crisply across the glazing in a powerful pattern of horizontal stripes of solid and void to make a stunning background for giant three-dimensional cut-out lettering spelling SCHOCKEN (later altered to an under-scaled *Kaufhaus Merkur*). As its southern end the facade was closed by a projecting semicircular stair-tower, the full height of the facade and entirely satisfying as a solid volume. But it was not a solid, and between projecting cornice-strips as closely spaced as the fins on a motorcycle cylinder, one glimpsed through to shoppers on the stairs within. Or with a change in one's position, or the fall of light, one got reflection instead of transparency, and suddenly saw the buildings on one's own side of the road, mirrored in extreme vertical distortion, transformed into ogres' castles and baroque cathedrals. It was everything eye-catching that advertising ought to be, but without cheapening the architecture; it was modernism with the popular touch, without cheapening the architect, and that – in sum – is what made Mendelsohn so hard to take for so long.

Erich Mendelsohn:
Schocken store, Stuttgart, 1927
Mendelsohn died in 1953, the first major talent of the generation of the eighties (born 1887) to leave the architectural scene. The rise of the Nazis having made his position impossible in Germany; he came first to England, where his major work was the Delawarr Pavilion at Bexhill, and later went to Israel and the USA.

JOHNSON WAX COMPANY BUILDINGS RACINE WISCONSIN

Frank Lloyd Wright

Worn down by the Master's own continuous rhetoric of earth, sky, rock, wood and agricultural virtue, most of us have come to accept a mythological picture of Frank Lloyd Wright as a sort of super-peasant, a primitive dolmen-builder suffused in bardic Welsh light. Certainly, the tribal encampment that he created under the hill at Phoenix, Arizona, and called Taliesin West, is the masterpiece of Romantic primitivism in modern architecture, but all through his career run buildings of conspicuous Machine Age sophistication, such as the Guggenheim Museum, and the king and queen of this persuasion are the Johnson Wax offices and their attendant laboratory tower.

The offices are near-enough contemporary with Taliesin West and could hardly be less like it. To the outside world, Johnson Wax presents blank brick walls, unpierced by windows, and rounded off with bull-nosed corners. But at the cornice (for want of a better word) the walls come to life with a glistening bulge of glass, for all the world like the chromium edge-trim of some primitive piece of Detroit car-styling. In functional fact, this glass trim is a piled-up system of parallel glass tubing that acts as a light diffuser, spreading light into the interior (and part of a membrane of similar tubes that roofs over most of the habitable interior space). Function notwithstanding, its appearance on the exterior gives a very strong sense of industrial styling, and the bridge unit that connects the different parts of the complex continues this theme by looking very like the chain-guard or similar part of some machine-tool: it is part of the image of progressive industrialism being worked up in the same period by US industrial designers like Norman Bel Geddes and Raymond Loewy. Through *their* efforts, in particular, it began to look like the beginnings of an all-American architecture in the buildings of the New York World's Fair of 1939. It came to nothing (for a variety of historically compelling reasons such as the war) . . . well, *almost* nothing, because the sub-style known as *Streamline Moderne* has left a few popular monuments to grace the American scene, particularly in California where extravaganzas like the Pan Pacific Auditorium

Wurdemann and Becket:
Pan-Pacific Auditorium, Los Angeles, 1935

104

look entirely at home in the Hollywood ambiance. But as a *national* style and a serious style it never made it. Johnson Wax alone survives as a testimony to what might have been.

It will always be remembered for the interior of the general office, a fantastic fish-tank roofed in concrete lily-pads and the membrane of transluscent glass. It was not Wright's first office, and he had earlier shown his preference for deep, top-lit work-spaces fitted out with office-equipment purpose-designed by himself. At Racine, the desks follow the bull-nosed aesthetic of the exterior, and have semi-circular ends, while the structural lily-pads on stems run all through the building, supporting not only gossamer glass ceilings, but also quite massive structures such as over-bridges.

When he came back to Johnson Wax, after the war, to design the laboratory tower, he decided to build the whole structure around a single lily-pad stem, and cocoon it in glass tubes – even round the bull-nosed corners. Alternating round and square work-floors are speared on a single central column like meat and vegetables on a *kebab* skewer. The circular floors are slightly smaller than the square ones and do not quite reach the outer skin which consists, as one sees it from outside, of alternating bands of brickwork and glass tubing on a square plan.

Although the corners are still snubbed off, as on the earlier block, the effect of the tall, banded tower is no longer primitive industrial design, but vaguely pharmaceutical or even electronic. The image of industrial progress had shifted and Wright with it, keeping an accurate finger on the pulse of technology even when pleading loudest for 'the natural house'.

Johnson Wax Co., office interior

University Engineering
laboratories, Leicester, 1963

Leicester laboratories, night view

Leicester laboratories, glass roofing

Wallace Harrison (executive architect): *UN Building, New York, 1950*

The spectacularly successful partnership of **James Stirling** (born 1926) and **James Gowan** (1923) came apart soon after Leicester was completed – though they got together again long enough to receive their joint Reynolds Aluminum Award for it. Subsequently Jim Stirling has had a great deal of international limelight, for University buildings at Cambridge, Oxford and St Andrews in Scotland (not to mention housing and industrial structures) while Gowan has received much less publicity, though his reputation stays strong among his fellow-professionals.

Facing page: Leicester general view

It is still best to come on it at first full dusk of a misty November evening – a mass of grey-blue translucent building stabbed by occasional patches of red or yellow light and entirely haloed by cooler light trapped in surrounding mist. Against the background of this luminous presence of architecture, silhouettes of people, students on a glazed spiral staircase, move like the inhabitants of a science-fiction fantasy.

Yet this is an entirely, strictly functional building, conceived and constructed within the penny-pinching constraints of post-war British university finance. Even by day it is compelling in the massing and contrasts of its forms, the reflectivity of its glass surfaces. And faintly baffling, for here is a work of manifest originality – nothing like it was built before, too many like it since – yet constantly evoking echoes of earlier Modern visions. There is nothing accidental in this: the architects gloried in the ambiguities arising from having to pack too much accommodation on an awkward site, which made radical forms unavoidable, while being sophisticated enough to understand exactly what historical echoes each radical form could stir.

Stirling and Gowan were major talents in the first generation of British architects to grow up in a world where Modern Architecture was not only an established fact of life, but was also being taught by thorough-paced scholars of international standing. Raised in the provinces they may have been, but there is nothing provincial about either; they know the international world of architecture, the unbuilt projects in forgotten magazines as well as the famous buildings that existed in concrete fact. For them, as for no earlier generation, being modern architects was a rich and various way of life, much less the pioneering battle it had been before 1939.

Because they were known to be erudite, many of the radical forms at Leicester were supposed by observers to reveal primarily aesthetic intentions, the desire to create an architectural jewel. Closer inspection reveals a devoted attention to functional need and economy, and even crudities that belie any gem-like ambitions. All that glass, carried in crude green-house glazing was simply the cheapest way at the time to clad so much volume of building and keep the weather out. Where it erupts over the walls of the lower workshops in diamonds like the surf of a frozen sea, it does so because the clients had asked for true north-lights in those areas in spite of the fact that the site required the block to be oriented at 45-degrees off true north. The resulting diagonal arrangement also made an ingenious and economical roof-structure possible – or so the architects claimed, relishing the fact that the whole thing *looked* completely wilful.

Between the lift and stair towers, the enclosing glass comes down like a frozen cascade that bounces forward at an angle whenever it arrives at a floor-level projecting further than the one above. Such shapes are almost impossible to draw in normal plan and section; an architects' perspective was transferred in chalk to the strong red brickwork of the flanking towers, the aluminium glazing bars were carpentered to fit on the scaffold and the glass cut accordingly. Such a casual, unimpressed attitude to metal and glass – sacred materials of modern architecture – bespoke a self-confidence in the face of that stern master 'The Machine' that was still rare in their own generation and virtually unknown before.

This can be seen as the first modern architecture that does not feel required to make heroic statements about the life, times and condition of Man in a Machine Age – and yet has far more to say on all those topics than many a high pronouncement like the UN building in New York. And if this is in the grand old phrase *architecture parlante*, a speaking architecture, then it speaks no rhetoric but the casual, real-life poetry that passes in conversation between airline pilots, skin divers and the like, discussing the life and workings of the machinery with which they share their lives.

UNITE D'HABITATION MARSEILLES

Le Corbusier

Le Corbusier: *Unité d'Habitation, Marseilles,*

The building for which a generation of architects waited almost a decade to give them a vital sign – the sign under which the real post-war architecture was to be born was Le Corbusier's *Unité d'Habitation* at Marseilles. Few projects have so accurately summed up the aspirations of their day, or so aptly; few can have so fully satisfied a body of disciples while disappointing their leader. Corb's disappointment stemmed from the fact that he intended to build a whole suburb in a cluster of such blocks, but politics and economics thwarted him in this particular case (and never gave him a proper chance anywhere else he tried). The satisfaction of his followers stemmed from the fact that it was the largest building completed as he had designed it (his UN project was being progressively coarsened and diluted) and because it showed that he was still making architecture anew.

The design, famously, called for a single compact rectangular block (descended directly from the *Pavillon Suisse*) containing apartments (mostly duplexes) and certain day-to-day social services such as shops and créches subsumed within the block. The scale was immense – over three hundred apartments - but was halved visually by expressing the double height of the duplexes by single openings on the outside, and putting the whole thing up on legs two storeys high (but looking only one). But something else happened to the scale in the course of design: originally conceived in terms of steel construction, the project had to be reconsidered from the ground up when the usual post-war shortages required

concrete to be used instead. Somewhere in the consequent delays and re-appraisals, the Master re-appraised also the aesthetics of reinforced concrete, abandoning the pathetic fallacy that this was a smooth precise machine-aesthetic material, and once more enquiring after its true nature. Instead of putting up a delayed pre-war building, he produced the first truly post-war one, monumental, not mechanistic, in the scale of all its parts.

Beginning with the legs – Le Corbusier's original concept of pilotis, as he called them, had been slim smooth cylindrical columns: at Marseilles they were massive pachydermatous stumps, tapering towards the foot and patterned all over with the impress of the plank-work of the shuttering in which they had been cast. So was all other concrete that had been poured and cast directly in place, and as the eyes of a delighted generation scanned the immense facades they saw concrete expressed by an architect almost for the first time as what it was, a moulded plastic material that could not exist without form-work in which to cast it. Further, Corb was visibly possessed of an aesthetic capable of dealing with this revelation: the surfaces showed the accidents of grain and knot in the unplaned planks that had been used; but the arrangement of those planks was no accident, and they had been laid in patterns as carefully as those of rusticated stone-work or a tiled floor. The first of the 'more crumbly aesthetics' of the fifties had been born.

This exterior was beyond dispute – there was some argument about what went on inside. Not about the two floors of social facilities half-way up, but about the flats themselves and the access to them. Each duplex apartment occupied the full thickness of the block on one floor, and half of it on the other, the deep narrow apartments being Chinese-puzzled in pairs around the central corridors that occurred on every third floor. Although both ends of the long floor of each apartment reached the outside air, even with a two-storey opening for the two-storey living-room, it was at the expense of a plan that was little better than a Bibby cabin,

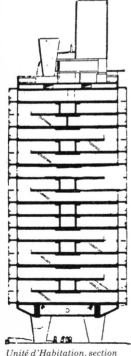

Unité d'Habitation, section

110

and the bedrooms in the long 'tail' of the flat were like a railway van. The access corridors, in turn though dignified by their creator with the name *rues intérieures* were, after all, little better than very long corridors without natural lighting. Characteristically, disciples who would hear no criticism of the master were soon at work improving both concepts, the improved apartment appearing in the LCC's Loughborough Road flats, the improved *rue intérieure* being partially exteriorised in the street decks of Park Hill at Sheffield.

But there were no second thoughts about the roof: even the rather gratuitous running track round its perimeter could be forgiven, forgotten in the state of aesthetic euphoria induced by this fantastic collection of functional megaliths, looking as if the children of giants had left their educational toys on top of the toy-chest. Seen against stunning views of mountain, sea and sky, the powerful shapes of the ventilators, lift-motor houses, play sculptures, platforms and stairs modelled by the sun, distilled for a generation the essence of 'the Mediterranean thing' and gave substance, triumphantly, to Le Corbusier's most famous definition of architecture – 'the cunning, correct and magnificent play of volumes brought together in light'.

Unité d'Habitation, concrete-work and pilotis
Unité d'Habitation, structures on roof

111

SEAGRAM BUILDING NEW YORK
Philip Johnson and Mies van der Rohe

LEVER HOUSE NEW YORK
Gordon Bunshaft of Skidmore, Owings and Merrill

ECONOMIST BUILDING LONDON

Allison and Peter Smithson

Mies van der Rohe:
Seagram Building, street front

**Skidmore Owings and
Merrill:** *Lever House, New
York, 1950*

113

Mies van de Rohe: *Seagram Building, New York, 1958 (at right, Lever House; centre, behind church, spire), the Racquet Club*

Philip Johnson's partnership with Mies van der Rohe on the Seagram building was the culmination of a master/pupil relationship based, in the first instance, on a scholarly admiration for Mies's work. Born in 1909, Johnson was almost forty before he even trained as an architect, but was already established as a critic and propagandist of 'The International Style' – a term he and the historian Henry-Russell Hitchcock had used to title their pioneering book on the aesthetics of modern architecture in 1933. His own career as an architect has been notable, but he may well be longest remembered as Modern architecture's sharpest wit and raconteur.

Skidmore, Owings and **Merrill** have only become the life, soul and epitome of big business architecture since the beginning of the fifties. An immense and reliable design-organisation even before that date, they still needed the undoubted talents of Gordon Bunshaft (born 1904) who joined the firm in 1946, to propel them to the forefront of the US and world scenes. With Lever House, in 1952, SOM and Bunshaft made a permanent mark, and entered on a career that transcended the limitations of big business architecture with such works as the US Air Force Academy at Colorado Springs.

Few architectural confrontations can be as fascinating, or as inscrutable, as that between the Seagram Building and the Racquet Club, facing one another across Park Avenue, and Lever House, oblique from Seagram but flanking the Racquet Club. The club is a most expert exercise in Beaux-Arts expertise by McKim, Meade and White, the American partnership who showed the French in the nineties that the Ecole des Beaux-Arts could be beaten at its own game of brilliant cliché-mongering. The Racquet Club is an *exercice de style*, and a skill in resolving visual problems that still strikes a chord in the architects of today.

Indeed, this trialogue is a discourse upon style in the grandest manner, in which the club puts down a basic proposition of traditional skill, and the other two discourse upon it in modern terms, derived from New York's first true prism, the UN Secretariat. UN was a European dream, the glass tower set between city and water, but planted in a townscape where skyscrapers are not a dream but a dirty commercial reality. The contrast between the ideal and the real set off

a brisk discussion on the aesthetics of the skyscraper in New York, and Lever and Seagram are the two most authoritative statements made, in built fact, in that discussion.

Gordon Bunshaft, the most brilliant designer to practice under the S O M umbrella, clearly set out to Americanise the European dream represented by UN, by imparting a dash of the puritanical – Lever is glazed all round, UN only on the main facades – and more conspicuously public-spirited: Lever is flanked by a little piazza 'dedicated to the public use'. Unwittingly or clairvoyantly, Bunshaft built a monument to an America whose existence could barely be sensed at the time: Eisenhower America, grey-flannel-suit America, with Madison Avenue literally only a block away. Its smoothly elegant solution was typically a compromise between two great creative ideas – Le Corbusier's vision of the tall slab with auxiliary structures at its foot, and Mies van der Rohe's vision of the all-glass tower. It gave architectural expression to an age just as the age was being born, and while the age lasted, or its standards persisted, Lever House was an uncontrollable success, imitated and sometimes understood all over the Americanised world, and one of the sights of New York.

But it was not what many observers believed it to be at the time, the last word in glass boxes. Over in Chicago, Mies van der Rohe was steadily developing his aesthetic (or was it a structural *rationale*?) of refined purity and rectilinear structural expression to a point of seeming logic well beyond the craftsmanly compromise of Lever House, and in the mid-fifties – rather suddenly, following some brisk internal intrigue among the Bronfman (Seagram) clan – Mies van der Rohe and his most devoted follower, Philip Johnson, found themselves designing an office block almost opposite Lever House.

But not dead opposite, and the first acknowledgement that the Seagram makes to any of its neighbours is to the Racquet Club. Standing back a little haughtily from the pavement, it takes care to share the same axis as the club, each standing symmetrically about the entrances that exactly face one another. This kind of formal good manners is Old World (not to say Olde Worlde) and quite un-American, and at every turn the Seagram reveals a kind of sophistication, an approach to urbanism, that has more in common with the Europe-oriented architecture directly in front of it, than with Bunshaft's unmistakably All-American Lever House standing catty-corner to the right. Lever stands well up to the pavement, but its slab is shoulder-on to the road. Seagram stands back, and front-on to the Avenue. Lever plays up glassiness, transparency and reflection, but Seagram, surprisingly, does not, emphasising instead the solidity of its block form, using a tinted glass that is darker and browner than Lever's, and bronze mullions that stick out from the facade as positively as pilasters, whereas the stainless steel glazing-bars at Lever barely ripple the surface, while the actual proportion of the tall narrow windows above the bronze spandrel panels (Lever has glass spandrels) recalls the fenestration of ancient palazzi.

Seagram and Lever have now been imitated to the point of tedium: 'square glass boxes' are a drug on the commercial market all over the world. Few of these imitators have had space, wit, or finance to pursue the piazza theme however: the Civic Center in Chicago by C F Murphy and Associates is the most noble exception to this depressing rule. If one seeks a true development of this concept of commercial public space it is most notably found in a work by two of Mies's more remote admirers. The crop-cornered towers that cluster around a raised pedestrian yard off St James's Street in London's clubland to form the premises of that grand old weekly paper *The Economist*, are the work of Alison and Peter Smithson. Their early reputation depended on a building that frankly imitated Mies – the school at Hunstanton – but their pursuit of their ever-admired master became less and less obvious, and at *The Economist* the tell-tale traces tend to lurk half-hidden, like the metal sections behind the stone facing of the columns.

Alison and Peter Smithson (born 1928 and 1923 respectively) are now the most internationally renowned husband-and-wife team working in Britain. Their reputation is based on a sparse roster of stern but controversial buildings, beginning with their Miesian-looking school at Hunstanton (see p 128). At the time the school was being finished they enunciated their philosophy as 'The New Brutalism' – a phrase which scandalised the Establishment (as it was meant to do) but enshrined a solid architectural morality to which students and younger architects turned for support not available elsewhere in the Fifties.

Alison and Peter Smithson: *Economist Buildings, London, 1964*

The groupings of these three towers (plus the matching monumental bay window on the never-before-exposed side wall of Boodles club) around a small piazza is – among other things – an attempt to develop the rather diagrammatic concept of fore-court demonstrated at Seagram into a more active contribution to the life and townscape of an area that is much more complex than Park Avenue. To move forward from Mies, the Smithsons were prepared to take a long step backward, to return to the sources of the Classical tradition that was always the backbone of Mies's designing. They know and love the sacred sites of ancient Greece; they have views on how and why they were planned as they were. Any visitor who stands at the foot of the steps that rise from St James's Street to the piazza and compares the grouping of the buildings with what he can remember of the view up to the Acropolis of Athens through the Propylaea may decide that what he sees could be the subtlest and craftiest piece of learning from Antiquity this century has produced.

PIRELLI TOWER MILAN

Gio Ponti and associates, Pierluigi Nervi and associates

Pirelli Building, roof-space

The reputation of **Gio Ponti**, born 1892, might well rest on his two beautifully detailed, but rather forbidding office blocks for Montecatini in Milan, but as editor of *Domus*, the monthly magazine of architecture and design, he has also propagated a more general image of Milanese high taste, that his own minor works, from the *Pavoni* coffee machine onwards, have done most to substantiate.

The reputation of **Pierluigi Nervi** seems to have been started after the second world war by some stunning photographs of his work by the American photographer G. Kidder Smith, and has been sustained ever since by his ability to do superlatively well one simple but difficult thing – put concrete vaults over enormous spaces. However, the Pirelli building in Milan (see p 116) shows that he could do other forms of structure with equal elegance and verve.

Italy's contribution to post-war architecture has been equivocal, and the critical assessment of many of her new buildings an uneasy exercise. One among the many difficulties has been the brilliant and formally perverse way in which Italian architects have underlined the falsity of the old equation between classical purity and machine technology that has bedevilled critics and architects alike since long before Le Corbusier made it eloquent in *Vers une Architecture*. Using traditional craft and pre-technological materials to produce supposedly mechanistic effects of smooth precision, the Italians coincided with Le Corbusier's *beton brut*, in accidentally undermining the symbolic values of the machine aesthetic, and reduced its stern canons to a formalistic game. Through all the resulting chaos and equivocations, Gio Ponti (everybody's favourite idea of an Italian artist-architect) has picked his way with a politician's skill, dashing off one sizzling design after another, many of them elegant trivialities, infuriating his more committed contemporaries. Then in 1959 he emerged as co-captain with Pierluigi Nervi of the team that conceived a building that proves him to be more than just an elegant trimmer to the winds of fashion.

The Pirelli tower, flanking the Piazza outside Milan's abominably rhetorical central station, remains one of the half-dozen towers of the fifties that matter. It re-stated all the Italian formalist equivocations over the machine aesthetic and yet gave that idiom new life as surely as the Seagram building. By one of those coincidences that make history improbable (though not as improbable as those surrounding the inception of the Seagram building) the impeccable structural logic of that phase of Nervi's career came into conjunction with certain formal preoccupations of Ponti's, and the world now has a building that is not formalist in spite of the care given to the study of its form, a tough-minded business building that is not just a rentbox, an advertising symbol that is not just a gimmick – and all this realised in a building that is manifestly a unified, integrated conception, in spite of the hours of sweat and horse-trading around the conference table that must have gone into its design.

The result is a building that looks razor-thin from end-on, and almost is: two main facades bend back to meet one another in plan, but never quite make it because an air-gap runs up the full height of the building just where the cutting-edge of the razor should be. Up the main facade run a pair of slender tapering columns, outward manifestation of Nervi's all-tapering structure within. At the top they carry a flat lid of a roof, but not visibly; the glass wall of the facade stops, and the columns are bent back inside, one floor below the roof, which floats above another air-gap. The three air gaps – down each end and one under the roof – give the tower the air of being a front, a back and a lid, on the point of joining to make a closed box, not yet closed, but for ever aspiring to do so.

It is that aspiration that Ponti wants the observer to see, for the Pirelli, like most great modern buildings, is a statement, a proposition ('slogan', says Ponti). As a counterblast to the endlessness and repetitiveness of curtain-wall architecture, Ponti wanted Pirelli to be read as a closed form: a *forma finita*. Because it is just on the point of closing it is read as closed far more securely than if it were finally shut and finished. It may not be a very grandiose ambition to create a building in which a fairly simple formal intention is to be read, but it is quite something to have achieved it in an idiom like that of modern architecture, which has produced so many buildings that will be forever inscrutable to the main in the street or piazza.

Pirelli Building, by night

Pirelli Building, plan and section

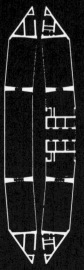

117

PAVILLON SUISSE CITE UNIVERSITAIRE PARIS

Le Corbusier

Pavillon Suisse, Paris, 1932

Come to terms with the *Pavillon Suisse*, and you have come a long way to getting to grips with modern architecture, for it contains much of the basic modern craft that has survived through every change of superficial style; its influence has gone round the world and altered modern architecture for good; and it combines all that is least superficial of both the new and the old in style.

From the past, it inherits one of the great ideas of the academic tradition, even though it was never made obvious there: this was the conception of a building as an assembly of volumes, each serving a specified function. The idea is as old as architecture, but Le Corbusier here made it eloquent and comprehensible by thinking not of a building, but of separate functional volumes, and designing the building by pushing these volumes together in such a way that their separateness and the fact of their assembly were unmistakable. The main function is to provide living accommodation for Swiss students, and this function is therefore served by the main functional volume, the dormitory. Its identity as a volume is underlined by lifting it off the ground on pilotis, so that one sees at once its actual size and content – the content being expressed by the forty-five room-size windows on the main facade – every square a room, every room a student. Where the pattern is varied at the topmost storey, this is because the content is varied: these are no longer standardised students' rooms but the sick-rooms and the warden's flat.

The other functions are auxiliary and are therefore served by volumes that are obviously accessory to the dormitory: by a stair-tower that, as near as dammit, doesn't actually touch the dormitory block, and by a sprawl of single-storey accommodation at ground level which, because it does not house the same standardised accommodation as the dormitory, breaks away also from the standardised geometry of that part. These two auxiliary structures are related to one another by the common feature of a curved wall on the stair-tower and a curved wall on the back of the students' common room, but their difference is at once emphasised by the fact that the

staircase wall is of smooth stone slabs, whereas the common room wall is of highly picturesque random rubble. This systematic alienation of the parts can be seen in one more symptomatic usage, where the porter's lodge, a forward extension of the single-storey structure, edges forward under the chassis of the raised dormitories – it looks suspiciously as if Le Corbusier has only done this in order to leave a gratuitously thin air-gap between the two at a point where a lesser man might have decided there was some structural gain in joining them up. Let no god, says Corb apparently, join what man hath decided to set asunder.

It is difficult to say which is the more compelling here: the brilliant demonstration of a hierarchy of functional parts with their functions carefully discriminated, or the emotive mixture of straight and curved, rough and smooth, romantic and classic – the 'two geometries', it has been called, or 'Corb's surrealism'. The ultimate surrealism of the design becomes most apparent when one realises that he has put his 'rustication' on a wall that does not support any upper storeys, (i.e. the common-room wall) while the smooth upper storeys, that would traditionally require a rusticated base, stand upon apparent nothingness; the chassis under the dormitories is cut back and rests on a narrow double file of columns under the centre of the block. Yet, even while traditional forms are being surrealistically flouted, the traditional and very French discipline of rational discrimination of functions has been fully honoured in the un-traditional composition of the whole.

The *Pavillon Suisse* has been described as one of the seminal buildings of the century, and it is true; its progeny are scattered all over the world, and number such distinguished buildings as Lever House in New York, the UN building, Lucio Costa's famous Ministry of Health and Education in Rio de Janeiro, and many other office blocks or public buildings that have kicked out a flurry of subsidiary structures from the foot of the pure prism of multi-storey slab. Corb's triumph, and the reason for his influence in this one work, was to have evolved a basic

Pavillon Suisse, bedroom side

architectural solution that was patently rational, yet left room for a great deal of personal freedom: a slab of logic raised on a base of free invention – a phrase which I freely admit to being a deliberate but (I hope) appropriate inversion of Corbu's famous dictum that technique is the base on which lyricism rests.

TWA TERMINAL KENNEDY AIRPORT NEW YORK

DULLES INTERNATIONAL AIRPORT WASHINGTON DC

Eero Saarinen and Associates

If it is true that 'form follows function' as the great Chicago architect Louis Sullivan proposed, then no two buildings should ever look alike, because no two functional situations are ever exactly alike. Most of the architects who have honoured Sullivan's precept have, in retrospect, appeared more concerned with making buildings *look* functional than *be* functional, and the evolution of a Functionalist Style meant that – say, in the guise of the International Style – they looked more alike than different. When an architect comes along whose style changes with changing functions, he tends to make the critics and pundits nervous, especially if the changing styles are conspicuously different, as with Eero Saarinen.

Famous son of famous father (Eliel Saarinen who transferred from Finland to the USA in the Twenties) he first practised an obviously Functionalist style, closely modelled on the work of Mies van der Rohe – very closely indeed in the buildings for General Motors at Warren, Michigan, – and then veered off into more and more idiosyncratic styles-for-the-job as his short career continued. Along the way, and in two different styles, he created the only two airport buildings of the post-war years that really stand out from the enormous number of passenger terminals and the like that have been put up in the last quarter century.

One of them, for TWA at Kennedy Airport, New York, captures better than any other the flavour of the high period of 'the Romance of Air Travel' and was meant to. The other, the single unified structure that houses all passenger services at Washington/Dulles grapples with the first intimations of airport problems to come.

TWA is now, if grudgingly, conceded to be as competent and imaginative a solution to the problems of the day (the late Fifties) as any architect ever achieved, *plus* a striking symbol of jet-age glamour. One says *plus* because the relation between function and symbol isn't all that clear. The earliest version of the design had a rectangular plan, much of which seems

TWA Terminal, entrance concourse

The career and reputation of **Eero Saarinen** (1910–1961) have become increasingly enigmatic in retrospect. He did not emerge from the aegis of his famous father, Eliel Saarinen, until he designed the General Motors buildings at the beginning of the fifties, after which his rise was as meteoric as his output was bewilderingly varied. Cut off in mid-career, he begins to look like a congenital experimentalist who had not found a personal idiom, and maybe was never going to.

Eero Saarinen: *Washington/Dulles airport, 1964*

to survive in the basement areas of the terminal; the vaulted superstructure, the so-called 'Bird' form, was designed later, after Saarinen had been to help judge the competition for the new Sydney Opera House, and there are some striking similarities between Jorn Utzon's vaulted shapes for Sydney and Saarinen's for TWA.

Be that as it may, the combination has always worked better than all the other terminals at Kennedy, and is graced by some subtle touches that are not pure styling or just aesthetic fancies. Thus the elevated passageways from the main building to the embarkation lounges are blind, slightly arched tunnels in the air; being blind they don't confuse you with the sight of all the other aeroplanes that are *not* the

one you're hurrying to catch, and being arched they offer a marginally more interesting and thus less anxious walking experience than if they were flat.

But it is still a fixed passageway, and the problem of such ever-longer 'fingers' reaching out further and further into the airfield to deal with more and more, bigger and bigger airliners, caused Saarinen and his advisors at Dulles to try a more radical solution. Everything that could be concentrated was concentrated, into a single monumental space under the huge hanging roof of the terminal. But instead of connecting this to the embarkation lounges by fixed passageways, they decided to put the embarkation lounges on wheels and let them cruise, ponderously, like vast motorised

covered-waggons, from the terminal to wherever the aircraft were parked. The present author, who has never missed a plane, has nevertheless contrived to miss the departure of one of the Dulles lounges!

In the form of the grand old British airport bus the solution is not new. The airport bus, however, is a half-thought expedient whose discomforts are depressing; the Dulles lounges are properly designed for their job and – like the TWA tunnel-in-the-air – both interesting and re-assuring. Of course Dulles is not perfect and the experience of incoming Customs is the same kind of plastic Kafka-esque trauma as anywhere else, but it is suspiciously *nearly* perfect. Suspiciously, because airports have proven to be the most transitional and transient building types of our time, always unfinished, always out of date. Did Saarinen-try to impose a final functional form on a process that ought to have been let run wild? Or could it be that the Romance of Air-travel has withered and the end of the Great Jet Adventure is in sight?

TWA Terminal, Kennedy Airport, New York, 1962

Washington/Dulles airport, mobile lounge

Joern Utzon: *Opera House, Sydney, 1973*

Crown Hall, Chicago, 1956

Mies van der Rohe's great scheme for the campus buildings at Illinois Institute of Technology was doomed to remain an unfinished fragment. Barely half a dozen buildings were done to his design and close enough together to reveal his original intention of an area planned and buildings built on a common grid of twelve-foot squares. Even so, there are one or two places where on walks out of one building, across a path, and into another with the feeling, not that one is traversing dead ground between separate structures, but merely an unroofed part of a continuous structure. This idea of a continuous structural space, roofed or unroofed, walled or unwalled, at will, has a respectable ancestry in the Modern Movement, but normally presupposes a given structural grid over the whole site before functional subdivision begins. Mies at IIT followed the more ambiguous (but also more practicable) approach of keeping the pre-existing grid in his head, and filling it out piecemeal with separate buildings that could equally well exist outside this specialised context.

Mies intended to vary this regular built/unbuilt space at certain points by buildings that did not so much contribute to the spatial system as float in pools of space within it. You can hardly sense this, as the scheme was left at the time of his retirement, because only part of the enclosure of just one pool exists; yet within it, raised by the height of a half-basement and differentiated from his other buildings by a larger scale in all its parts, floats Crown Hall, his American masterpiece, the holy of holies, the architectural school.

Effectively, it is a single room, big enough to contain the entire school, and free of columns because the structure is carried in giant trusses clear over the roof, which is hung from them. Entry is by a flight of steps placed classically and symmetrically in the centre of each long side, and all necessary interruptions of the continuous space are grouped closely about the central axis that connects the doors. There are no other permanent subdivisions, and the few there are never rise much above man-high, so that one has, from all parts, an uninterrupted view of the high continuous ceiling, and thus an overwhelming sense of the sheer size of the room and – *via* the all-glass walls above eye-level – of its continuity with the world-space outside.

The idea of placing the whole school in a single continuous space has caused alarm in some quarters (one might do better to cavil at the way the Industrial Design department has been crammed into the basement) but the alarm only shows how ignorant we are of the performance of buildings of this scale and type. The lack of obvious acoustic and visual privacy is a matter of complete indifference in this enormous room because it is enormous. No one is conspicuous, because his activities are insignificant in comparison with the room and the visible world outside. But because the world (or, at least, the sky) outside is visible all round, it is not distracting – anyone who can read in the park can work in here. And because the nearest sound-reflecting surface is usually the ceiling eighteen feet above (and that is sound absorbing, anyhow) private conversations are not immediately bounced back at one's neighbours and eaves-droppers, and may be effectively inaudible three desks away. Inhabited by serious-minded near-adults, not screaming teenagers, Crown Hall is a crystal casket of meditative calm.

It is also an object lesson in how to be a modern architect. Mies's chosen means of expression were sheets of glass, and steel I-beams. Materials that ought to be the commonest stock-in-trade of a Machine-Age architecture: glass because it is the ultimate controller of weather, excluding everything but light, a fine membrane between two climates, one hostile and uncontrolled, the other man-made and adjustable; the steel I-beams because they approximate most closely to the ideal of a non-existent structure, no other material having such a spectacular ratio between reliable strength and visible substance. With these materials Mies created a functional space that is orderly, but with such ideal simplicity that order is made manifest only by the structure – floor, upright stanchions, roof – because there is

nothing else to see. And because there is nothing else to see but a great space, visual attention, when it shifts from sheer space to smaller things, can only fix on the details. These are few, and almost all of them are concerned with the problem of mating glass to I-beams, the precise collocation of subsidiary metal sections that secures the glass, weatherproof, to the edge of the steel. This simple working detail was half of Mies's architecture ever since he began to build in America, and he never solved it.

Not because his joints don't work, but simply because he never found the final and perfect joint. He never could, of course. Human, he could think of a better architecture tomorrow; also, he lived in a most sophisticated technological culture, which might offer him a better component tomorrow. This is the splendour and the misery of modern architecture, for whether or not the architect believes in perfect, ultimate solutions, he still feels the moral obligation to work his brain to the bone producing best-possible solutions for today, which may be superseded with the first post tomorrow. Mies was not the only modern architect to quote 'God is in the details', and it is in details such as those of Crown Hall, perfected today but perfectible tomorrow, that one sees what kind of God is modern architecture's.

The immanence of that detailed Godhead was immediately manifest. As soon as the IIT style appeared in Mies's work it was irresistible. The American architects Philip Johnson, Eero Saarinen and Gordon Bunshaft (of Skidmore, Owings and Merrill) fell so totally under his spell that they were affectionately called the 'Three Blind Mies'. In Chicago a whole 'New Chicago School' grew up under his shadow. Even outside America the influence was almost unavoidable – two of the most consciously reformist modern buildings in Britain in the Fifties clearly acknowledge this divinity of detailing: the Secondary school at Hunstanton in Norfolk by Alison and Peter Smithson, and the air-terminal at Gatwick by Yorke, Rosenberg and Mardall.

Crown Hall, interior

Crown Hall, detailing of main frame

Alison and Peter Smithson: *secondary school, Hunstanton, 1954*

Yorke Rosenberg and Mardall: *Gatwick airport, 1959*

129

CLIMATRON ST LOUIS MISSOURI

Murphy and Mackey

The fame of Buckminster Fuller was a phenomenon of the fifties when – the right man at the right time – he came suddenly to the forefront as Mister Number-One Space-Age-Designer. The acclaim was as justly earned as it was superficially given: given because his dome-shaped structures and their supporting non-rectangular mathematics caught the fancy of a generation that was bored with square architecture and ready for curves; Fuller's or Ronchamp's made no difference. But Fuller's emergence in the space decade was also just, because he considered the problems of human shelter in terms as rigorous as those forced upon the designer of a space capsule, and had been considering it in those terms for something like thirty years. The geodesic (great circle) domes were only one arm of his assault upon these problems, and it is a sad sick comment on the way we humans run our environment that fully-engineered versions of these domes have usually been employed to provide fit habitations only for radar installations, propaganda, pigs and rare plants.

Yet the Climatron at St. Louis is a fair representation of his aims and ideas, working, as is usually the case, through the minds of other men who have licensed patents from him. A space-age greenhouse as surely as the Crystal Palace was a steam-age greenhouse, the Climatron is a spidery lattice dome full of carefully controlled climate, designed by the St. Louis architects, Murphy and Mackey (and it won them a major architectural prize). Fuller himself is on record with visions of gigantic domes soaring over garden environments which they shelter from the hostile climate outside, but the Climatron goes one better than this and maintains twelve *different* micro-climates to suit different sorts of plant ecology, requiring different admixtures of heat and humidity.

It achieves this result without any internal partitions, but simply through controlled flows of cooling or warming air, plus controlled local as well as general supplies of water. More, it does this without excluding the full natural sunlight through the transparent plastic that covers the dome, though at the cost of a fuel consumption that the ordinary greenhouse

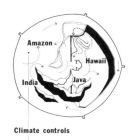

Climate controls

warm air tunnel   underwater passage

Climatron, diagrammatic plan and section

Do-it-yourself domes, Drop City, Colorado, 1967 onwards

operator could not contemplate, and a battery of electronic aids that he could not afford. There are those who admit that the Climatron is a sort of earthly paradise, but deny that it is architecture, merely gadgetry. One can reply, on Fuller's behalf, that permanent structures are only one of the means by which an architect creates human environments today: electronics and other 'non-architectural' studies are further means to extend our control over environments, and if architects cannot make them part of their art then the human race may decide to disencumber itself of the art of architecture, just as it has disencumbered itself of the arts of witch-doctors and rain-makers.

Which could prove ironic, because much of the promise of Fuller's comprehensive design strategies, along with his domes, has since been usurped by the kind of primitive soul who salutes the sun and makes peace with nature in desert dawns, and scrutinises signs in the sands and grasses for guidance on the business of the day. Because of his radical critiques of the established orders of architecture, technology and society, Fuller became one of the heroes of the dissident architecture-students of the Sixties; furthermore he himself had gone out of his way to demonstrate – in the Third World and elsewhere – that once his geometries had been understood they gave a 'mind over matter competence' that worked as well with low and intermediate technologies as with that of space-travel . . . and given all this he was interested

to find himself the guru and patron of the 'intentional communities' who, from 1966 onwards, began to opt out of the affluent and pollutive society, and to people the deserts of the American south-west.

Like inflatable structures, domes and space-frames *à la* Fuller became part of the environmental furniture of the Alternative Culture. Some have a distinct air of poetic vengeance on the 'Established' culture they reject.

Drop City in Colorado, as much a sacred site of the Counter-culture as was Haight-Ashbury, had its domes cobbled together from colourful sheets of pressed steel hacked from the roofs of wrecked cars with the paint still in place, fenestrated with odd-shaped glass from car-windows and its public spaces adorned with sun-worshipping sculptures made from old driving-mirrors. So, with time circling around in quest of its own revenges, it is most possible that some Peace-saying hippie, gazing speculatively at the firmament on the night of the last Apollo-mission and apostrophising its crew with 'Moon-men, what are you *doing*?' would have done so from the door of a rude shelter constructed according to the precepts of that same Buckminster Fuller who had also been the hero of the preceding, science-worshipping generation – for whom a moon-shot would have been an occasion not of sarcasm, but of reverence.

Buckminster Fuller's life and works contain sufficient incident, surprise and change of scene to make a film epic inevitable. Born in 1895 he had a conventionally disorderly college career, served in the US Navy and became interested in problems of human environment in the mid-twenties. Since then he has been free-booting on the frontiers of architecture, preaching a radical and scientific attitude to building design that architects find simultaneously fascinating and repellent. Official recognition did not really come until his domes for the US Marines in the early fifties, since when he has been one of the USA's leading cultural exports.

*Harumi apartments,
Tokyo, 1957*

134

Brutalism, as a going philosophy of architecture, always had more aspects (sociology, town-planning, for instance) than the single one that has caught the public fancy, namely, the use of unfinished materials 'as found', and for some reason that the wise men of architecture have not yet elucidated, all aspects of brutalism seem uncommonly likely to occur in Japan. If ever a building was superficially Brutalist and Brutalist in depth as well, it is the big apartment block at Harumi by Kunio Maekawa; its publication in 1959 really startled the world. Superficially it is Maekawa's manifest pleasure in handling large lumps of stuff that makes it Brutalist – the great splay-footed concrete piers that hold it all up, the shameless great industrial water-tank on the roof, the cryptic numerals *15* in figures about six feet high on the end wall, the massive balcony fronts. Maekawa had passed through Le Corbusier's office briefly, and all these usages are Corb-inspired divergences from canonical Corbusian usages, such as one finds in the work of others regarded as Brutalists.

Yet more to the Brutal point of view is the bold, not to say blatant way in which the building expresses its structure and its operation: every fourth floor is simply a giant box beam, partly for structural reasons, partly to house duct-works and communications. This external rhetorical drama of the building as an operating mechanism is complemented by an extraordinary tenderness for the living habits of the tenants; each flat is effectively a traditional Japanese dwelling – *tokonoma*, mat-module-planning and all – slotted into place in the giant pigeon-hole system of the structure at large. Again, there is the attempt to make the building a unique and identifiable place, dear to all the Brutalist connection, and vindicated here by the local street-fightin' men adopting its corridors and stairs for a suitable venue for their nocturnal rumbles. When people rally to a place on purpose (even if the purpose is illicit combat) you know it has in some way established itself, perhaps because the designer is an architect who approaches people in a specially empathetic way. Social empathy is a mood that holds together much progressive

Harumi apartments, end elevation

In the Fifties, **Kunio Maekawa** was often spoken of as a new name in Japanese architecture, but he proved to be no stripling either in years or achievement. Born in 1905, he travelled widely, studied in Europe and was working for le Corbusier as early as 1929. With such a background he was not only the *doyen* of Japanese modernists, but the guide and mentor to many of the younger generation, like Kenzo Tange.

architecture today – on this accounting, Park Hill in Sheffield, so different from Harumi in detail and bulk, reveals itself as a close cousin of Maekawa's block. The mixture of heroic scale and domesticity, exposed mechanics and permissive sociability, are present in both. The mental infrastructure of modern architecture is international even where the forms are uniquely local.

CHURCH AT IMATRA FINLAND

Alvar Aalto

Vuoksenniska church, detail of roof

A brilliant beginner, **Alvar Aalto**, made his first international impact with the Paimio sanatorium in 1930, when he was just thirty-two. He justified his world reputation with the memorable Finnish pavilions at the Paris Exhibition of 1937, and the New York World Fair of 1939. His status as a legend was confirmed when one of his finest early works, the library at Viipuri, was supposedly destroyed in the Russo Finnish war, before the rest of the world had been able to get a proper look at it, and his later works have continued to reinforce the solid structure of his tremendous reputation.

Too many of us respond to the mention of Scandinavian architecture with a stereotyped mental image of exquisite craftsmanship in teak and brick, harnessed to a conception of architecture so middle-of-the-road as to be entirely characterless. Yet, in all honesty, we know that the Baltic nations abound in architects of tremendous character, natural extremists: Jorn Utzon who conceived the sail-boat vaults of Sydney Opera House; Ralph Erskine of the 'underground' shopping centre at Lulea in the Arctic; Arne Jacobsen, most pure and extreme of European machine-aesthetes, as witness his town hall at Rodovre.

And Alvar Aalto – the Finn on whom superlatives fall as naturally and plentifully as Arctic snow: giant, genius, form-giver, master-builder, wizard of the northern forests, and every word of it deserved. For forty years, Aalto has been the quiet man of the Big Four; his name did not always spring to mind quite as rapidly as those of Mies, Le Corbusier or Gropius, because his work is harder to classify and does not lend itself quite so readily to the accepted public-relations techniques by which architectural reputations are maintained. But Aalto was always there, and his buildings unmistakably of our time but never entangled with our fashions, command a respect that is unlike that afforded to the work of the other masters.

There is, about most of his buildings, an unobvious, devious, obtuse and almost grudging charm that gives nothing away at first sight – Aalto can be a bit like that himself – but yields more and more to whoever is prepared to work away at it. His Vuoksenniska church at Imatra seems, at first look, to turn from the viewer and hide, humping its copper roofs defensively against the sky and lifting cautious windows, like watchful alligator eyes, above the white substructure in which it seems to burrow. This unyielding exterior has much to hide, since the interior volumes do not tally with the exterior bulk, though both express a plan and section that gives a narrow high apse at one end, and a broad flat tail at the other, where the entrance is. Each of the alligator eyes corresponds to a hump in the internal ceiling (not reflected in the roof-forms) over one of the three separate divisions of the interior.

What makes these divisions separate is a couple of sets of sliding partitions that can be rolled out of the walls of the processional porch of the tower. From the moment they begin to roll, everything is pure Aalto. They head straight across the nave, but in traversing the centre aisle each door passes through one of Aalto's favourite devices, a pair of coupled columns standing right in the aisle, and then the door curves round to follow the plan of the outer (but not the inner) window. Not only are the windows double, with the inner glazing sloping in to meet the humped ceiling, but the slightly arched structural beam that spans the nave beside the door tracks goes straight on when the door curves round. Absolute visual chaos seems inevitable, but Aalto avoids it, not by some radical simplification such as Corb might have introduced, but by piling on further complications: between the curving door-track and the straight beam he inserts two delicate, almost millinery, curved vaults with slatted ventilators in them.

It works – and the fact that it works is as Aalto as the blunt non-communicative exterior; the effect as Finnish as the exquisite folk-paintings on the boarded ceilings of Finland's wooden country-Baroque churches. This too is part of Aalto's special genius: his ability to strike a resonance with folk traditions without ever copying them or being sentimental, without ever ceasing to be his own immensely sophisticated and hard-headed self.

Alvar Aalto: *Vuoksenniska Church, Imatra, 1956*

Arne Jacobsen: *Town Hall, Rodovre, 1955*

137

HIGHPOINT 1 AND HIGHPOINT 2 HIGHGATE LONDON

Lubetkin and Tecton

From the Penguin Pool onwards, the contribution of the Tecton partnership was a major part of the total momentum of the movern movement in England.

Down to the Hallfield development in Paddington, every building was a battle won, and they remain as numinous as the monuments of heroes – none more so than the Highpoint complex in Highgate. With Highpoint I, British modern architecture became man-size and internationally visible, and Le Corbusier set the seal of his approval on it by dubbing it the first 'vertical garden city'. By the standards of modern architecture it was an unconventional block, a double cross in plan, and its windows were far from gigantic or wall-size, but on the ends of the arms of the cross they were graced by little balconies whose scrolled fronts scream 'thirties' even while they pass muster, still, as a convincing solution to the problem of finishing-off a particular kind of facade. Where the block is most convincingly modern-movement, however, is in the bold and plastic treatment of the entrance hall that runs most of the depth of the ground floor, and demands comparison with the first stirrings of modern (equally Corb-inspired) architecture in Brazil. The Corbusian inspiration need cause no surprise: his ideas went everywhere through the agency of intelligent men, like Lubetkin, in revolt against their academic training. His professionalism and bred-in-the-bone classicism, his rationalism and his rhetoric caught them where they lived and their own work took fire from it. In the entrance hall of Highpoint I the British saw for the first time that modern

architecture could be a full-blooded visual art, as well as a conscience and a social programme.

All this was too much for the slow-witted citizens of Highgate, and when the Highpoint organisation wanted to develop the site next door (to prevent its misdevelopment by someone else) they found that the powers of aesthetic control that had lately been vested in local authorities as a defence against bad architecture could be used to prevent any kind of architecture at all. There ensued a comedy of desperate manoeuvres worthy of Ben Jonson, in which the local 'planners' were patiently flannelled into accepting, one by one, all the features of the new building, under the impression that quite different matters were under dispute. The outcome was not, perhaps, the best conceivable building for the site, but it is a worthy consort for Highpoint I, and its double-height living rooms were the right sort of next step forward.

But Highpoint II also has a front porch that has taxed the patience of the friends of modern architecture almost as much as Highpoint I taxed the minds of the Highgate villagers. The form, structure, applied lettering and practically everything else about that porch are as resolutely modern as anyone could have wished in the thirties, but where there ought to be slender steel columns to hold it up, there are – of all things – casts of one of the Erechtheum caryatids, from the British Museum. It was (and is) completely indefensible, but it clearly comes from the same classics-based professionalism as gave us the rest of the scheme, and the architects have defended it with the same forensic brilliance as they used to make rings round the villagers' aesthetic objections to Highpoint I. Now that the increasing sophistication of us all has made Lubetkin's classicism more obvious and his modernism less so, this Hellenic pin-up seems less of an affront to progress than it once did; no more than a classicist's sign-manual . . . until you think of the fantastic self-confidence needed to do it at a time when your strongest supporters had only just cured themselves of regarding Greece as the be all and end all of artistic excellence . . .

Lubetkin and Tecton: *High Point II, Highgate, 1938, the caryatid porch*

High Point, entrance hall

High Point, Highgate, 1935

139

PARK HILL SHEFFIELD

**City Architect,
J. L. Womersley**

**LCC Architect's
Department:** *Roehampton
housing, 1958*

The City Architect of Sheffield
under whom Park Hill was
designed was **Lewis
Womersley** (born 1910), one
of the distinguished tribe of
architect/civil-servants who
helped build the high
reputation of British
government-built
architecture in the Fifties and
Sixties. Others were Robert
Matthew and Leslie Martin
(London), Donald Gibson
(Coventry, and Nottingham in
the period of CLASP) and
C. H. Aslin, pioneer of the
Herfordshire programme of
prefabricated schools, and
thus the true begetter of
CLASP, SCSD (see p 152)
and a host of other systems
all over the world.

Ever since the war we have had the curious
spectacle in Britain of social programmes that
were grandiose in scale, being realised in penny
packets of architecture. Very good packets, at
their best, like the isolated towers of the LCC's
Roehampton development, scattered through
the established greenery of their beautiful site
like off-white Monet girls in an impressionist
garden. But where, demanded a generation
regarding with despair the coy scale of the New
Towns, where is the building that is as big as
the sociology?

Sheffield gave the answer, but not until the
beginning of the sixties. On a straggling,
sloping site at Park Hill, the City Architect's
department rehoused an entire slum clearance
area in one gigantic building – the first of the
megastructures, you might say – whose sheer
size would be sensational anywhere in the
world,(three times as much accommodation as
the Unité at Marseilles) and yet the gross social
statistic is less important than the concept of
sociability that is the backbone of the whole
design. The concept is made manifest by a
system of broad street-decks that run like a
literal backbone, right through the building, as
it snakes and forks its precipitous way down the
slope; a drop equivalent to nine storeys in
height. The decks that make it possible to get
from one end of the building to any of its four
other ends without going down to ground level,
are big enough to admit tradesmen's pedestrian-
controlled delivery-trucks and stray bicycles,
but they are free from normal-death-dealing

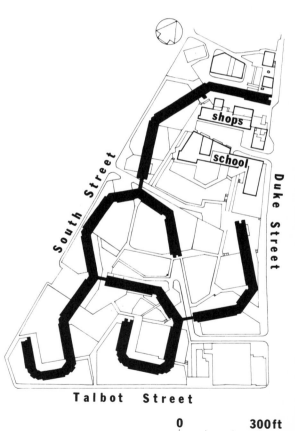

Park Hill, general plan

Sheffield City Architect's
Department: *Park Hill
housing, 1961*

141

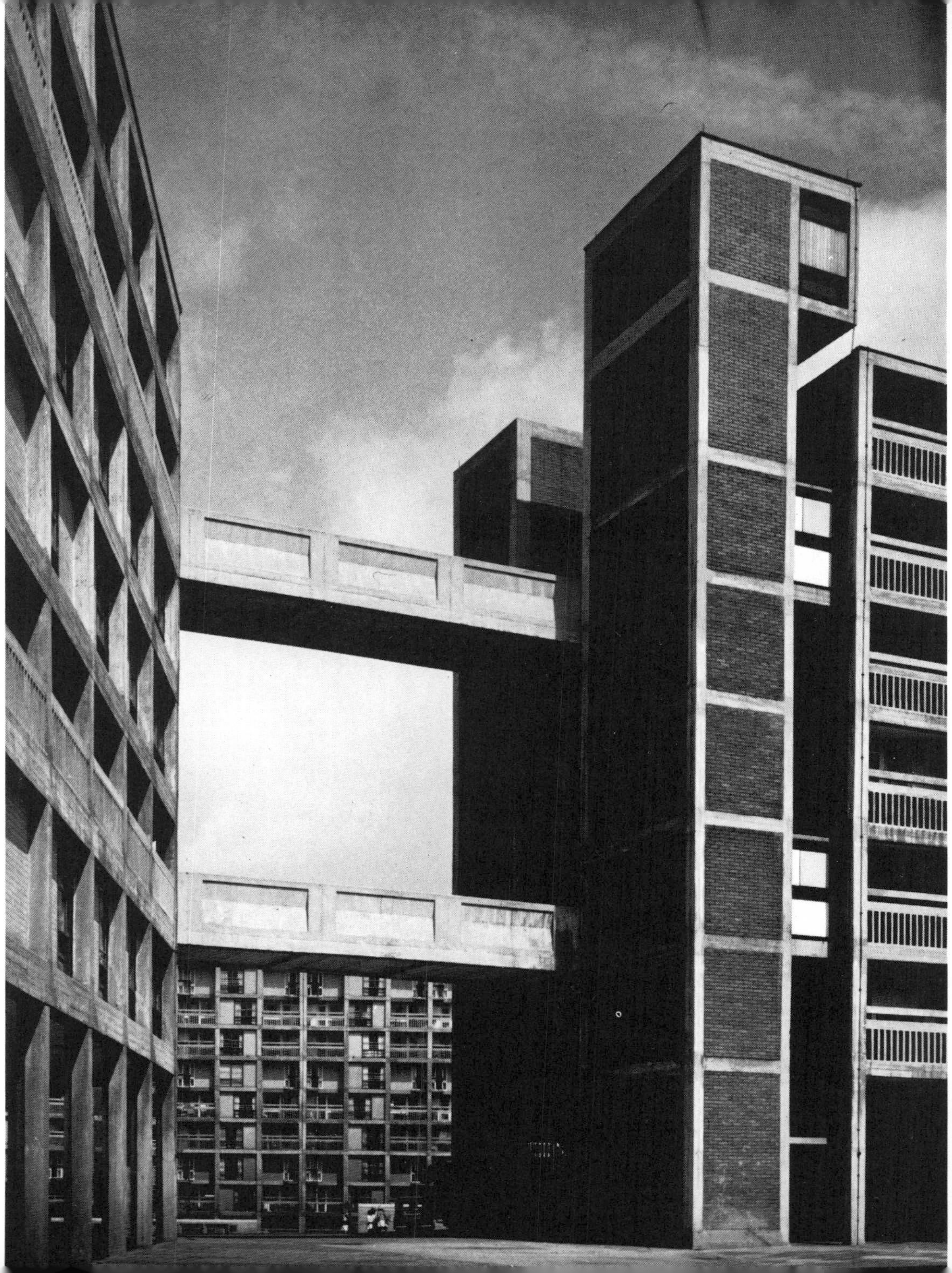

Park Hill, stair towers and bridges

types of wheeled traffic and, since the doors of
all the apartments open on to one or another of
the decks, they promised a street-like channel
of communication and social encounter as well –
at corners and lift-lobbies and other such
points, mums could gossip, teenagers do their
things, dads could hash over union affairs and
the football pools – though what happens
chiefly in practice is that mini-tricyclists use
the long straights between these points as
improvised drag-strips!

You can walk for ten minutes along one of these
decks, as it threads its way first along one side
of the block and then the other, alternating
stunning panoramas of the city with close views
into interior spaces partly walled in by the arms
of the block. The architectural detail with which
one is immediately surrounded is plain and
blunt; not all of it will stand very intensive
study in isolation, but when you stand back
from the block at the down-hill end and peer up
at the soot-grimed cliff of habitation from
the depths of the Sheaf Valley, the details
dwindle into insignificance, even though the
sense of human presence does not.

Opinions are divided, even so, about what
happens to the human presence on this scale.
Serious critics like Lewis Mumford believe the
scale of the block to be inhumanly vast, others
decry the social concept (which meant so much
to the young architects who conceived it) as
mere 'matiness'. Only time and research would
really show whether either objection is
justified, and the results of the research that
has been done seem, as usual, fairly ambiguous.
But there can be no doubt that Sheffield has
acquired (and is still proud of) a building
that is in a class by itself, realised in the teeth
of a site that would have deterred less men than
the boys of the project team responsible: Jack
Lynn, Ivor Smith and Frederick Nicklin.

However, their true mastery of the design seems
less powerfully manifest at the extremes of
scale – the sheer size of the site, or the close
domesticity of the decks – than in the middle
range, where such designs so often go wrong.
Park Hill reveals its inmost secrets with the

Park Hill, a pedestrian deck

greatest architectural conviction at the three
points where the block bifurcates, which are
also the only three points where access roads
are allowed to penetrate into the pedestrian-
sacred precincts within. To accommodate these
multiple functions, one limb of the block halts,
with the customary pair of vertical circulation
ducts (one for lifts, one for stairs) that happen
wherever a block ends. But at this juncture, a
horizontal circulation duct – a bridge carrying
a street deck – leaps from the landing serving
the lift and stairs, across the access road to
connect with the street deck at the same level
on the two divergent limbs opposite. At these
points, especially where as many as three
deck-bridges are superimposed across a single
gap, Park Hill states unequivocally that it is a
gigantic structure held together by pedestrian
circulation – that is, men, women and children,
walking along, on the scale and at the pace of
the human race.

HABITAT MONTREAL

Moshe Safdie and Associates

TOWN CENTRE CUMBERNAULD

Geoffrey Copcutt
(Hugh Wilson,
Architect-Planner to
the New Town)

Moshe Safdie and
associates:
Habitat, dwelling-boxes

According to the accepted mythology of Modern Architecture, all the great exhibitions since that which produced the Crystal Palace in 1851, should be expected to produce equally revolutionary buildings of one sort or another. Statistically, the actual box-scores of most exhibitions suggest that their performance doesn't support the myth; worse, that some of the buildings only look revolutionary and flatter to deceive – the Trilon and Perisphere at New York 1939, or the Atomium at Brussels 1958. Nevertheless, the legend waits for someone to exploit it, even now, and at Expo 67 in Montreal, a bright young Israeli student at McGill University exploited it to build his dream of megastructure. Well almost; *Habitat* as built was not exactly Mose Safdie's final-year thesis – what got built was tamer and less innovating, but it came remarkably close to being a concrete realisation of the kind of gigantic housing project that was on many a student drawing board all over the world in the mid-Sixties.

Even if tamed, it remained a controversial design. It cost a lot of money, but the expense was supposed to be justified on the grounds that its mode of construction – pre-cast conccrete apartment-sized boxes made on the ground and lifted into place by a giant crane – was an experiment that might not otherwise have been made in North America. But didn't it look fabulous, this craggy ziggurat sitting on the edge of the water? Wasn't the lack of privacy deplorable – almost every balcony and many living room windows were overlooked by other apartments? Yes, but weren't the views of Montreal terrific? So what, the rents were ridiculous . . . and so on.

Never mind. It made Safdie and it helped to make *Expo 67*. With its separate and standardised room units clipped together at will and at whimsy – it seemed – and served and supported by external systems of lifts and walkways, it was the epitome of the current dream in architecture: the megastructure. There were other megastructures around at the time, some of them at Expo . . . or were there?

People seemed to recognise a megastructure when they saw one that season, but most would have been hard put to define one. It wasn't just a large building; the Vertical Assembly Building at Cape Kennedy was admired for being the largest building in the world, but no one thought it was a megastructure. If anything, the concept was easier to define in un-built forms – the wild graphic fantasies of Plug-In Cities, Walking Cities, Computer Cities of the English Archigram group, vast urban complexes made of habitable capsules large and small that could fit *ad hoc* and subject to revision, into elaborate structures affording support, service and communication.

No one was ever going to build them. Habitat got close, but closer still was the town centre of Cumbernauld in Scotland. Bang on time and right in style, it derives from an improbable, perhaps wrong-headed, but heroic decision. Instead of treating the town centre as public space with buildings round it, the planners decided to let Geoffrey Copcutt design a single building and put the public spaces inside it. Stradling a dual-carriageway motor road along the ridge which forms the backbone of

Habitat Montreal, 1967

Moshe Safdie, unknown architectural student turned overnight international success with Habitat, was born in Tel Aviv in 1936. The construction of Habitat was the due reward for the relentless pursuit of an ideal conceived in his last years as a student at McGill, and developed in the teeth of all the disappointments and obstructions known to architects (and they are many!).

Cumbernauld New Town, this enormous structure of indeterminate and apparently unfinished form houses all the shops, offices, pubs, hotel, city departments, health facilities of a complete city.

Among its myriad supporting legs are car parks and loading docks, above them more parking, then the lower shops, then the main concourse and bigger shops; higher still, more specialised shops, cafes, public offices, then professional offices, finally a thin cresting file of apartments commanding enormous views southwards. The exterior is all bumps and excrescences, different kinds of glazing and roofs and public platforms and walling systems, some solid and permanent-looking, some seemingly temporary, waiting for the design to decide what to do next.

In fact there won't be much next; what has been built so far is a small fraction of Copcutt's original design, but it seems to be all that's going to be built in this particular mega-mode. It remains one of the Monsters of the Modern Movement; like it or not, you have to admit the sheer nerve and vision that caused it to be built. Inhuman is it? Why then is it the only new town centre in Britain that doesn't die in the

Geoffrey Copcutt/
Cumbernauld
Development Corporation:
*Town Centre, Cumbernauld,
1967*

*Cumbernauld Town Centre,
model*

*Cumbernauld Town centre,
shopping area*

*Cumbernauld Town centre,
general view*

evening when the shops shut; why are there people about at all hours even on the Scottish Sabbath? The answer is that unlike all the other town centres it is a much more desirable human environment than the rest of the town – because it is the only place the citizens can get away from the stinging gales that blow up the ridge and the rain-squalls they drive before them even in the summer!

BRASILIA
BRAZIL
Oscar Niemeyer,
Lucio Costa and others

CHANDIGARGH
EAST PUNJAB
Le Corbusier
(architect for the Capitol)

Oscar Niemeyer:
*Parliament Buildings,
Brasilia, 1960*

Unlike Cumbernauld, Brasilia was the most conventional version of an architect's dream – to create a new city on an unspoiled site; it's what architects dream of in novels! Better still, capital-city splendours were built into the contract from the beginning. Chandigarh falls short of this dream because much of the city had been laid out by other hands before Le Corbusier set foot on the site. He got his way in the corner reserved for capital splendours, but could only fiddle with the city. Against this, Brasilia has complications of divided command: Oscar Niemeyer was the head man, and designed the government buildings, but the city-plan is the work of Lucio Costa, who won the right to this most coveted of jobs in open competition. And Costa could hardly be Niemeyer's subordinate since he was his boss on the team that designed the celebrated Ministry of Health in Rio that launched the Brazilian school on its triumphant progress towards – Brasilia.

But at least, the style in which both men are grounded is the same, was invented by them for the Ministry on the basis of some sketches by Le Corbusier who was briefly consultant on the project. In Brasilia that style of contrasting geometries, one square and regular, the other irregular and curved or angular, has been pushed to systematic extremes. It happens not only in the buildings themselves, but in the relations of building to building, even in the town-plan, where the hard straight line of the 'governmental axis' slashes through the vague free-hand curve that outlines the residential area. Along the roads, straight or curved, are ranged blocks that exhibit the contrasted geometries as a matter of course, plain and square in bulk form, but raised on fancy pilotis and crowned by free-form roof-structures. In the Fifties the accomplishment with which the Brazilians handled this style was the envy of the world, now it is as commonplace as the way the Americans use curtain-walling. However, Niemeyer's use of the two geometries is no more commonplace than Mies van der Rohe's use of curtain walls.

In the Presidential palace, he condensed the two

It seems to be supposed that **Niemeyer** (born 1907) gets all the credit while **Costa** (born five years earlier) does all the work; or that Niemeyer has inspiration, while Costa has only application. Yet Costa won the right to lay out the town of Brasilia with a scheme whose overwhelming recommendation was that it took off from a stroke of inspired imagination. What seems more likely is that Costa, sheltering under the edge of his official appointments was in a position to implement imaginative gestures on behalf of other people, such as calling in Le Corbusier as consultant on the Ministry of Education in Rio.

149

Oscar Niemeyer: *Chapel and Palace of the Dawn, Brasilia, 1959*

geometries into a single rectangular box, its immensely spacious interior laid out with simple grandeur and without curved walls, while the second geometry appears, with tremendous effect, only in the leaping curves of the swan-like arcading that supports the loggias that shelter the palace walls all round. Against this, the Parliament building represents a more conventional reading of the Brazilian style, but pushed to its last extremity of elaboration. The single tall slab has twinned, and become equivocal: is it two slabs of office accommodation standing close together, or is it a single administrative block split down the middle? At all events, the old easy simplicity and clarity are gone, and replaced by a sophistication that makes earlier Brazilian architecture look naive (which it often was, bless its progressive aspirations!) Under the twinned slab, and at right angles to it (as usage dictates) lies (as usage also dictates) a horizontal element terminating not in a single auditorium (as in the universal prototype, the Ministry of Health) but crowned by two council chambers, one in the form of a low dome, the other in the same form but the other way up; a saucer. But if both are chambers (one for senators, the other for deputies) how can they be truly functional and yet such different shapes? Both in practice are fairly loose fits on functions that, after all, are determined by human relationships, not mechanical operations, and the complementary forms are justifiable as architecture of a grand, rhetorical simplicity.

And, functional or not, they are still modern architecture as we have known it, clean, crisp, precise (and all that jazz), the product of the kind of sweeping self-confidence that is necessary to clear a slum or found a capital. Nothing could be more different than the government buildings at Chandigarh. There, it looks as if Corb had read that the late work of a great master is broad, rough, inscrutable and deceptively simple, and had decided to play it by the book. Comparisons between Chandigarh and late Beethoven quartets have already been voiced, further corn about Rembrandt and Michelangelo is to be expected. Yet the fact

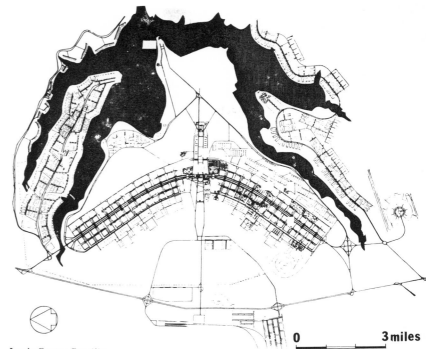

Lucio Costa: *Brasilia master-plan, 1956*

0   3 miles

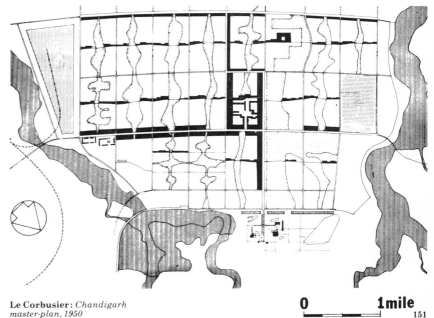

Le Corbusier: *Chandigarh master-plan, 1950*

0   1 mile

151

Le Corbusier, *Secretariat,*
Chandigarh, 1956

Le Corbusier: *Secretariat*
and Parliament, Chandigarh

remains that the simplicities, almost crudities, of Le Corbusier's design for the Law Courts, with a row of justice-boxes simply shacked up under a concrete sunshade makes Niemayer's most sophisticated work look brash; the jazzy breaks in the rhythm of the regular fenestration of the Chandigarh secretariat, caused by the intrusion of double-height ministerial rooms, make Costa's ritual separation of parts look jejeune; and Le Corbusier's planning, conceived in terms of vast rectangles of earth pegged out with obelisks, makes Costa's plan for Brasilia look only a little more subtle than borough surveyor's work.

Only, Costa was right and Corb was wrong, as far as one can see. The conception of planning that groups the buildings of the Capitol at Chandigarh is very very old indeed; it belongs to the peasant-powered world before machine technology; a world where mere horizontal extent was laboriously impressive to the walking serf, and the mere presence of geometry was numinous proof of the triumph of the human will over natural chaos. A couple of successful Five Year Plans, or a flush of democratic affluence in the Punjab, will make nonsense of this before the buildings have had a chance to acquire the air of hoary reverence that makes the piddling courts of the Louvre impressive even to those who normally live at freeway scale. But Costa has planned Brasilia in terms that would be generous even on a community that had two Cadillacs in every garage instead of a bus-stop on every super-block. His module is circulation, and the highest drama of his town is where major traffic streams meet, fuse and resolve themselves again in his multi-level town-square and bus-station. Compared with this, Corb's Chandigarh seems to hang in an historical vacuum waiting for some unexpected turn of events to validate its extraordinary conception – an Acropolis on the site of a suburban supermarket.

CLASP SCHOOL MILAN
Nottingham County
Architect's Department

SCSD PROTOTYPE PALO ALTO CALIFORNIA
Ezra Ehrenkrantz and
Robertson Ward

Committes, group-practices and other forms of collective design are so often blamed for bad architecture that it has become the current cant that they can never produce any good architecture at all. I have been told that all Britain's post-war schools must be bad because they were designed by 'committes of civil servants'. Yet, on one of the rare occasions that a British, 'committee-designed' school was exposed to international competition, the international jury awarded it the biggest prize they had to offer and then up-graded the prize because they felt it was not as big as the virtues it was meant to celebrate. That *Gran Premio con Menzione Speziale* at the 1960 Triennale (three-yearly exhibition of architecture and design) in Milan went squarely where it belonged – to the Nottinghamshire architect's department, and the CLASP system of construction – of which more anon.

The fact is, obviously, that there are bad groups and prize-class groups, and there are different kinds of good architecture. If architecture is only allowed to be good when it starts as a thundering statement of an individual personality, then not even a prize-class design-group can produce it. But if good architecture starts with a human need clearly understood and imaginatively served, then a group big enough to undertake research, before design, is able to provide good architecture. There is no magic about this: the group has to consist of real talents; it has to be organised to get the best out of them; and its relationship with the outside world must be good, too. In the now-established English post-war tradition of 'development-group design' that relationship starts with research into the requirements of the users; in schools, into adapting the planning to the most advanced teaching methods. But Nottingham is also a member of CLASP – the Consortium of Local Authorities Special Programme – formed to pool research and information on structures, cost-cutting, bulk-buying etc., between a group of Local Authorities in the North Midlands. Out of the special requirements of these authorities (such as the consequences of mining subsidence) came a constructional system, a kit of parts,

that is now the CLASP thumbprint internationally, and was largely responsible for that *Gran Premio.*

Among prefabricating systems it is one of the world's wierdest – the pioneers of modern architecture saw prefabricating systems as ruthlessly logical, simple, cut to the minimum of components, and this view has become the ideal. But the CLASP system, which is real, not ideal, is only as logical as it needs to be, only simple enough to get by, and by no means minimal: it often offers more than one way of solving a problem, such as the cladding of a wall. The range of choice (almost unknown in other prefabricating systems) could give the ratepayers better schools for less public expenditure, but it also gave quite a lot of architects a better chance to get on and design a building that serves the needs of the user, without having to spend hours drawing out details. The user of CLASP had at his fingertips a set of ready-designed details that combine together naturally into architecture.

And that isn't magic either; a lot of mental sweat went into the first creation of the system to make sure this would happen, and a lot of continuing research was needed to make sure it went on happening as the system was developed further. In Milan, it worked beautifully, and world design leaders could see, for instance, how the framing of the window automatically tidied up the otherwise ragged edge of the tile-hanging. Maybe this was not architecture in the sense of Le Corbusier's classic definition of 'magnificent, cunning and correct play of masses brought together in light', but it was an architecture that many nations were prepared to adopt; not only were variants of CLASP devised for use in Germany and Italy, but before the mid-Sixties there had appeared SCSD (Schools Construction Systems Development) in the USA. To be exact, SCSD is not a direct descendant of CLASP (as are later British systems like SCOLA) but a product of the same British background since the architect primarily responsible, Ezra Ehrenkrantz, worked in England and gained wide experience in British research-based

Ezra Ehrenkrantz and
SCSD: *prototype school, Palo
Alto, 1962*

Nottinghamshire
Architects' Department:
*CLASP system school,
Triennale di Milano, 1960*

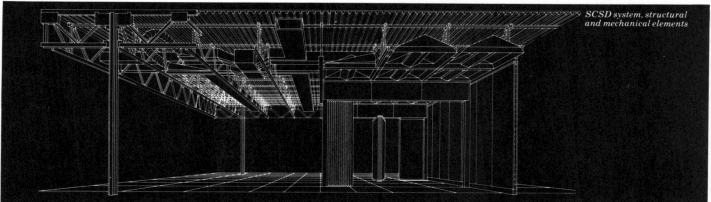

SCSD system, structural
and mechanical elements

architecture of the CLASP period before
returning to the USA.

The result is an architecture that goes against
the American grain in some respects, and with
it others. *Against:* the need for school districts
to sacrifice their independence and pool
resources to create enough finance; *with:* the
high degree of technical ingenuity in the
mechanical services packed into the roof.
Against the grain: a commitment of capital so
big that only manufacturing giants like Inland
Steel could afford to bid competitively, cutting
out the smaller local firms; but *with:* the
decision to let local architects devise the
external architecture as long as they used

Robertson Ward's ingenious and economical
roof system.

As a result, SCSD schools for better or (usually)
worse look much less alike than any one
generation of CLASP schools, and none of
those actually built by Schools Districts look
anything like Ehrenkrants's prototype. Walled
entirely in glass with its metalwork all dark,
that prototype sits among the California
Eucalyptus on the fringes of the Stanford
campus, and – since there is little to see in this
version that isn't Robertson Ward or Inland
Steel – says 'Made in Chicago' as clearly as if it
was written on it in words, or signed by Mies
van der Rohe!

BAUHAUS DESSAU

Walter Gropius

156

The present state of the Bauhaus is the enduring shame of the modern movement. Not that anyone can do much about it while Germany remains effectively halved and it lies beyond the remains of the Iron Curtain: decrepit, damaged, derisorily restored, its famous walls of glass still reduced in part to small square windows, in a 'provisional' brick skin. But if it were possible to do anything to mend its ravaged face, there are many who would be glad to have it off their consciences.

Why be so concerned? For two reasons. Firstly it is a sacred site, where Walter Gropius gave architectural and institutional form to a concept of design education that has changed the world, and inspires, enrages, supports and depresses design-teachers even today a half-century after he first began to rough it out. The first Bauhaus, which he founded at Weimar in 1919 was already dedicated to the heart-and-hand concept of learning by doing, education through knowledge of materials and tools. At Dessau the concept could be extended to include the reasoning mind and machine production. The new buildings there had a machine-shop as well as studios, and the architecture school – as befitted the eagles' nest of a new age that Gropius savoured as sharply as the Futurists did – was on a bridge spanning a road between two blocks. This was not an ingenious necessity inspired by a difficult site, for the ground had been wide-open and suburban when Gropius began to design; the relationship of building to road was of Gropius's own making, the road was there because he put it there. A manifesto building, then, for a motorised age.

Secondly, it was more than a manifesto, it was a masterpiece: the first really big masterpiece of the modern movement, the full powers of the new architecture deployed for the first time on a scale too big to be dismissed as mere domestic eccentricity. Gropius presented to the world a large, multi-purpose structure cast entirely in the new idiom, and so convincingly that there could no longer be any doubt that this idiom was an architecture in its own right, as surely as Gothic or Georgian. But the mastery

exhibited by Gropius at this master moment of his career, goes deeper than the mere management of a style. The Bauhaus buildings at Dessau, in their original condition, were modern right the way through. The functional grouping of the parts may appear loose, with the building hooking out into the landscape in three right-angled arms, but there is no suggestion of the building falling apart visually. From all aspects – and it is meant to be seen from all sides – the separate elements are seen to group themselves satisfactorily in a manner that never fails to reveal the underlying formal order of the whole, the difference of construction and fenestration revealing the functional order that underlies the forms, and nowhere more powerfully than in the all-glazed wall of the workshop block.
Sigfried Giedion has called it a space-time composition, revealing itself only to a moving observer as he circulates round it, but such an observer should also move *through* it, because as he passes under the celebrated bridge, he will find himself at one point in the middle of a balanced symmetrical composition, with identical and equal entrances facing one another on opposite sides of the road, serving identical stairs lit by identical windows. It so happens that these two 'separate but equal' entrances served the Dessau Technical School on one side, and the Bauhaus proper on the other, thus reintroducing a 'snobbish distinction between artisan and artist' that Gropius had once tried to abolish – just one of the little political compromises by which Gropius kept the Bauhaus together through thick and thin, and far less important than what the symmetry itself seems to symbolise. This piece of antique formality must be some kind of ritual gesture to the ancient gods of order and discipline, for which symmetry is still the most eloquent symbol we have, for the Bauhaus is, above all others, the building in which Gropius dedicated himself and his followers to the concept of the disciplined service of a functional order, and proved the concept to be as expressive and architectural as any exercise in architecture or expression for their own sakes. It is a shrine to the belief that the Machine Age is good.

0   50m

Bauhaus, site plan

SCHINDLER/ CHASE HOUSE LOS ANGELES

Rudolph Schindler

Schindler-Chase house, Los Angeles, 1923, courtyard

Rudolph Schindler, born 1887, and **Richard Neutra**, born 1892, were both Viennese and led closely linked careers, Schindler going first to the USA and helping Neutra to follow him. In California they shared an office and worked together on one of the most radical projects for the Palace of the League of Nations (though like Le Corbusier's it was rejected). They quarrelled and split up at the end of the Twenties, but were re-united after a fashion by sickness in the early Fifties when they shared a hospital ward. Schindler, however, lived only till 1953 and died before his present international reputation was established, whereas Neutra died loaded with honours, as the saying goes, as late as 1970.

Modern architecture might have taken a number of different roads – like de Klerk's in Amsterdam – that were later abandoned when the Movement settled for the Teenage Uniform of the International Style. If there is one architect who explored all these roads (or more than anybody else, at least) it was Rudolph Schindler, domestic architect extraordinary in California. He was one of a fairly close connection (Eric Mendelsohn, Richard Neutra) who were attracted to the US by their admiration for Frank Lloyd Wright. Schindler, who worked briefly for Wright, was one of those who decided to stay and invited his fellow-Viennese, Neutra to join him in Los Angeles. Neutra was always a fairly straight, though immensely skilful, practitioner of the International Style and his famous Health House is one of the monuments by which the style is now defined. Schindler too practised the International Style, but as one of a dozen or so well or ill-defined alternatives borrowed or invented by himself. This variability has bothered historians, who have tended to fasten enthusiastically on the house he built at Newport Beach for the same client as Neutra built the Health House – enthusiastically because it is an astonishingly early yet rich and inventive example of the International Style, fully to be compared with Rietveld's Schroder House or Le Corbusier's villa Cook of the same years. It has its place now in the history books, but on the spot in California, surrounded by the ingenuity and diversity of his other work, being International Style looks less important than being an original Schindler.

For he was one of the originals of our time, and it's all there from the very first house he built as an independent designer. Conceived as a double house, for his own family and that of a close friend, Clyde Chase, it belongs to no style, started no fashion; it has to be approached and valued on its own terms. Its construction looks odd, though there is local precedent for it – large concrete slabs were cast flat on the ground and then tilted up in place to form the walls. They taper thinner towards the top, and are separated by narrow slots, sometimes glazed, that look like mediaeval firing slits but

are just there to stop the slabs fouling one another edge-to-edge on being tilted into place.

This air of defence and fortification, however, is only on the public sides of the house, towards the street. All the rest of the construction is in wood and quite light – the roofs, the glazed sleeping porches on the roofs, and the sliding glazed walls that look into the system of half-enclosed courtyards that are what the design is really all about. The scale is tiny, but this hardly matters when nearly all the habitable spaces open freely into these courts. The construction techniques are clever throughout, but also have a slightly improvised air. The whole thing has the freshness of a brilliant and highly trained European talent learning to relax and enjoy himself in a California whose golden legend had not yet been smirched by smog, and learning to marry traditional American hammer-and-nail construction to European artfulness in the arts of managing space.

It's all quite difficult to see nowadays, because the descendants of the original planting shown on Schindler's designs have pretty well taken over the scene, and made a habitable jungle of what was once a plot of shrubby semi-desert land. But it is to be emphasised that this is a *habitable* jungle; house and vegetation have grown together in a living tribute to one of the greatest domestic designers of the present century.

Schindler-Chase house, plan

Richard J Neutra: *Lovell (Health) House, Los Angeles, 1930*

CHEBEL SOOTUM TEHERAN PERSIA

Brown and Daltas

*Chebel Sootum,
near Teheran, 1960,
entrance and interior*

Near Teheran, steel-framed, designed by two US architects and a British engineer – this ought to have been International Style if ever any building was. It isn't; it looks like a fairy palace of some sort, and in strict Functionalist theory that's right, since the client was a Persian Princess. The Chebel Sootum – Palace of the Forty Columns – is one of those buildings that seems to be unknown to the many for exactly the same reason it is known and cherished by a few. It was a successful rebuke to all those who, in a curious phase of uncertainty among American Modernists around 1960, tried to pursue the same Oriental fantasy for the wrong reasons.

As embarrassed architecture-fanciers later tried to forget extravaganzas like Philip Johnson's Shalimar- style pavilion in New Canaan, Ed. Stone's Embassy in New Delhi, and Yamasaki's Gothicisms everywhere, the palace of Princess Fatimeh was undeservedly pushed into the same limbo. Looked at again ten years or more later, it comes up fresh, honest and convincing because it remained astonishingly true to those fundamental precepts of Modern Architecture that the others had been trying to set aside.

It's a structure of shamelessly exposed metal – clusters of steel tubes rise from a splayed base and, twelve feet above ground, spread to form the carrying ribs of vaults made of special lightweight brick, a commonplace material transformed by subtle-coloured surface glazes. And that – plus a floor or two, balustrades, water and windows – is about the whole of the building; couldn't be simpler or more charming.

Given the state of the local building industry this delicate fantasy was also practical and cheap. The heavy oriental whimsies being erected in the US at the period were neither practical, nor cheap, nor very convincing. Chebel Sootum was all these things without trying to be, because it concentrated on the original business of architecture – Firmness, Commodity and Delight; in case you'd forgotten.

Chebel Sootum, entrance side

Chebel Sootum, plan

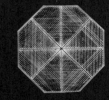

PHILHARMONIE
BERLIN
Hans Scharoun

NATIONAL
GALLERY
BERLIN
Mies van der Rohe

Hans Scharoun:
Philharmonie, Berlin, 1964

162

Modern architecture – the better part of it, in many senses – was made in Berlin. Later-to-be-famous names from many countries were to be found in the roster of assistants in Peter Behren's office before 1914, and learned their business there. Later, when the Masters of Modern Architecture got together for the exhibition at Weissenhof that defined the International Style, half of them seemed to be Berliners. The city had a lot to give the budding movement; its architectural traditions were grave, disciplined, professional, devoted to public service high and low, local and national. It bequeathed to us all the idea of modern architecture as a painstaking search for quality in public design.

The city's best buildings have always been public ones; the professionalism with which even minor municipal works were done has become a legend. The tradition of severe classicism in which they were conceived proved extraordinarily durable, rooted in what seemed an immutably stable professional society. It lasted until Hitler; he liked classicism but he destroyed the solid bourgeoisie who had built Berlin, and the post-war vicissitudes of peace have continued the erosion of this once great tradition. Recent architecture in East Berlin has tended to look social and efficient (and not always well built) and in West Berlin improvised if clever (and not always well built either). In the two Berlins there seems to be no one left around who can still do Berlin architecture. In the mass of construction that has piled up in West Berlin there is only one locally designed building good enough to sum up the situation: the Philharmonie. Hans Scharoun, its architect, was a Berliner, yet, but for decades or more subtly out of step with the others, rejoicing in romantic informality. Externally, the Philharmonie looks like a vast solidified tent, its roofs and walls drooping down in a variety of materials that are allowed to meet, edge to edge, with a nonchalance that can be breathtaking, and so can the way it places its windows.

Inside matches outside, illogical-seeming staircases and random-looking structural

Philharmonie, Berlin

Philharmonie, Berlin, auditorium

163

columns lacing a vast free-form foyer from which one eventually ascends to the auditorium – deviously. In walked fact the route is less

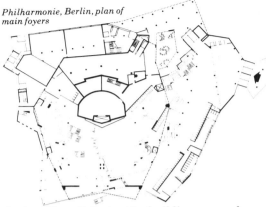

Philharmonie, Berlin, plan of main foyers

devious than it looks, the building conceals a great deal of common human sense and proves that visual disorder does not necessarily imply functional disorder. The auditorium itself is apt to look like a chaos of intersecting planes, light fittings, suspended acoustic panels, and slabs of tiered seating sloping around in disordered array. But viewed calmly from your seat, it reveals a symmetrical layout with reasonable sight-lines to the orchestra platform. In many senses, the style and functioning of the Philharmonie is part of that passion for atonement by which honest and decent Germans strove to put the Nazi years behind them. Putting the Nazi's classical preferences behind them as well, they turned to that alternative German modern tradition of Expressionism. In the process they missed the true, pre-Nazi tradition of Berlin architecture, and it is doubtful if anyone left in the residual Germany after the cataclysm could have done that kind of design with a clear conscience and a steady eye.

But across a couple of hundred yards of car-parks and uncertain terrain from the Philharmonie stands a building that affirms the survival of the true Berlin style in exile. The new National Gallery was designed by Mies van der Rohe in Chicago, but it is all Berlin. He had been out of the city thirty years when he came to design it, but he had conserved in Chicago

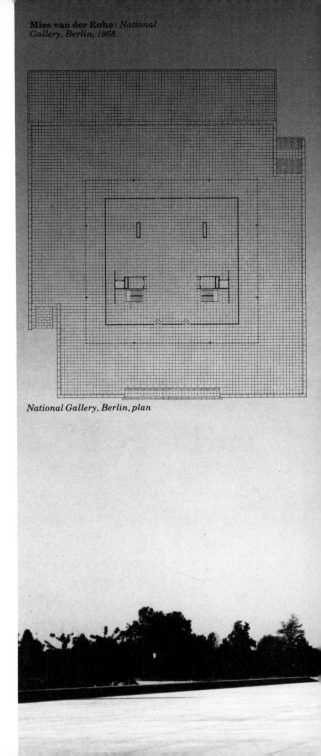

Mies van der Rohe: *National Gallery, Berlin, 1968*

National Gallery, Berlin, plan

National Gallery, interior

the essential professional ethic of the society that had been destroyed in its native town.

The Museum is grave, rational and disciplined, imbued with the public decorum and classicism of the Germany of Goethe, Beethoven, Schiller, Bach *und so wieder*. And the Berlin of Karl Friedrich Schinkel, founding father of that great municipal tradition. Yet it is ultimately less backward-looking, less sentimental than the Philharmonie. It is a bare, spare statement in steel and glass about the definition of a usable fragment of universal space. It may evoke conscious echoes of Schinkel's *Altes Museum* of 1824, but the long unsupported cantilever corners of the roof beyond the two skinny columns on each side have nothing to do with any past tradition in museum design. In fact, Mies so extravagantly flouted that

tradition in creating this glass box that he has been accused of un-functional irresponsibility as much as Scharoun at the Philharmonie. How can one exhibit works of art in an environment that is clear glass all around and without a single solid wall within? Depends what you mean by a work of art – small cabinet pictures probably would get clobbered, but large works of modern sculpture, Op and Pop art, seem to thrive in it. Small cabinet works – and much other good stuff – is well looked after in the almost windowless galleries buried in the hundred-metre-square podium on which the visible pavilion stands.

This still leaves some viewers feeling uncomfortably that Mies had indulged himself above ground, and buried those functions in which he wasn't interested. Yet, in Berlin, that looks an insensitive judgement. This is a formal statement – a *mal* (as in *Denkmal*) or monument – made also in thanksgiving to a city that understands formal statements, even if it has received few of equal gravity and civility in the last quarter-century. Addressing himself appropriately to an unrepeatable situation, Mies made a gesture that was unrepeatably traditional and modern at once.

So, in its own way, does Scharoun's Philharmonie. No view of modern architecture in the Age of the Masters can be complete if it cannot embrace both the classical and the romantic, the plain and the devious, the fancy and the naked. All these, in the service of function, are within the range of modern architectural possibilities. All you need is nerve, and those old Masters had it!

National Gallery, Berlin, night view from the sunken sculpture court

INDEX

CREDITS

**Acknowledgements are
due for the illustrations on
the following pages:**
2 Portraits of the masters in
old age:
Mies Van der Rohe, Frank
Lloyd Wright, Walter
Gropius, Le Corbusier:
'The Architectural Review'.
4 Materiel Habitable:
Aldo Loris Rossi.
5 Plug-in City:
Archigram architects.
10, 11 School of Art,
Glasgow:
Glasgow School of Art.
13 Museum of Modern Art,
New York:
Museum of Modern Art.
15 Fagus Factory, Aalfield:
Verlag Gerd Hätje.
16 Parliament Building,
Chandigargh:
Rondal Partridge.
16 Century Bank, Los
Angeles:
'Architecture & Urbanism'.
19 Maison Citrohan:
Courtauld Institute.
20, 21 Villa Savoie, Poissy:
Lucien Hervé.
22 'Le Modulor':
Faber and Faber.
23 St Paul's Church, Bow
Common, London:
'The Architectural Review'.
23 Chapel, Ronchamp:
James Stirling.
24 Vertical Assembly
Building, Cape Kennedy:
'The Architectural Review'.
25 Eames chair:
Hille of London;
Rietveld chair:
Museo von Amsterdam;
Breuer chair:
Aram Designs.
27 Housing at Pessac,
France:
David Hicks.
30 Garage Ponthieu, Paris:
Peter Collins.
31 Turbinenfabrik, Berlin:
Courtauld Institute.
32 Water Tower, Posen:
Deutsche Werkbund.
33 Factory, Luckenwald:
The Architectural Press.
33 Civic Centre, Saynatsalo:
Architectural Association.
33 Farm buildings, Garkau:
Architectural Association.
34 Generating station:
Museo Civico, Como.
34 Villa Cook, Boulogne-sur-
Seine:
Courtauld Institute.
35 Neissenhof Exhibition,
Stuttgart:
Museum of Modern Art.
36 Monument to Karl
Liebknecht and Rosa
Luxembourg:
Museum of Modern Art.
37 Fundamentalist,
Suprematist Elements:
Courtauld Institute.

38 Ministry of Education,
Rio de Janeiro:
G. E. Kidder-Smith.
39 House, Mathés:
Courtauld Institute.
42 Notre Dame, le Raincy:
H. Roger Viollet.
43 Town Hall, Hilversum:
Architectural Association.
44 Bridge at Schwandbach:
Visual Publications.
44 Fiat Factory, Turin:
*'European Architecture
of the 20th Century'*.
45 Aircraft hangar, Orvieto:
'Architecture of Aggression'.
46 Monadnock block,
Chicago:
Chicago Heritage Committee.
46 Villa, Bourg-la-Reine:
Chicago Heritage Committee.
46 Flats in Rue Franklin,
Paris:
Lucien Hervé.
47 Jahrhunderthalle,
Breslau:
Cement and Concrete
Association.
47 Cosmic Ray Pavilion,
Mexico:
Cement and Concrete
Association.
48 Milan Triennale
cardboard domes:
Foto Studio Cavall.
48 Motel cabin prototype:
Jean Bowry.
50 'Girl with Mandoline':
Courtauld Institute.
50 'Battle Evolving in Space':
Courtauld Institute.
53 Foyers, Royal Festival
Hall, London:
Hillary Harris/
'The Architects' Journal'.
52, 53 Guggenheim Museum,
New York:
Solomon R. Guggenheim
Museum.
54, 55 Farnsworth House,
Fox River:
Hedrich Blessing.
56 Crystal Palace, London:
Dell and Wainwright
'The Architectural Review'.
56, 57 Eiffel Tower, Paris:
H. Lacherry.
59 Water and Power
Building, Los Angeles:
Julius Schulman.
60 Johnson House, New
Canaan:
The Architectural Press.
62 Fremont Street, Las
Vegas:
Desert Supply Company.
67 Flats in Zaanstraat,
Amsterdam:
Courtauld Institute.
69 Schröder House, Utrecht:
Brattinga, Amsterdam.
72 Span housing, Ham
Common:
Sam Lambert/
'The Architects' Journal'.
72 Clusterblock, London:
Denys Lasdun & Partners.

70, 71, 73 St James Place
Flats, London:
'The Architectural Review'.
75 Factory, Bryn Mawr:
Tempest (Cardiff) Ltd.
75 Factory, Blumberg:
Egon Eiermann.
75 Factory, Merlo:
Reyner Banham.
76 Eames House, Pacific
Pallisades:
Charles Lee/Chris Rubke.
78, 79 Ford House, Aurora:
Kenchiku Planning Centre.
80, 81 Penguin Pool, London
Zoo:
Michael Reid.
83, 84 Town Hall, Kurashiki:
Ch Hirayama.
84, 85 Communications
Centre, Kofu:
Osami Murai.
86 Laboratories,
Philadelphia:
Cervin Robinson.
88, 89 USAEC inflatable
theatre:
The Architectural Press.
89 Inflatable in tv studio:
Julian Cooper.
90 Novocomum Block, Como:
The Architectural Press.
91 Monument, Como:
Courtauld Institute.
92 Casa del Fascio, Como:
G. E. Kidder-Smith.
93 Casa Guiliani-Frigerio,
Como:
Giuseppi Terragni.
93 Asilo Sant'Elia, Como:
Giuseppe Tarragni.
94 Casa del Girasole, Rome:
A. Cartoni.
95 House on the Zatteri,
Venice:
Dr. Ignazio Gardella.
96, 97 Robie House, Chicago:
The Architectural Press.
99 House at Huis ter Heide,
Utrecht:
Rijksroorlicht Ingschienst.
101 Schocken Store,
Stuttgart:
The Architectural Press.
102, 105 Johnson Wax Co.
buildings, Racine:
Corning Glass Works.
104 Pan-Pacific Auditorium,
Los Angeles:
Hazel Cook.
106, 107, 109 Leicester
University Engineering
Block:
'The Architects' Journal'.
108 UN Building, New York:
United Nations
Organisation.
110, 111 Unité d'habitation,
Marseilles:
Lucien Hervé.
112, 114 Seagram Building,
New York:
Cervin Robinson.
113 Lever House, New York:
J. Alex Langley/SOM.
115 *'Economist'* Building,
London:
'The Architectural Review'.

116, 117 Pirelli Building,
Milan:
'Domus'/Pirelli.
119, 120 Pavillon Suisse,
Paris:
Lucien Hervé.
122, 123, 125 TWA Terminal,
Kennedy Airport, New York:
'The Architectural Review'.
124, 125 Washington/Dulles
International Airport:
'The Architectural Review'.
125 Opera House, Sydney:
David Moore.
126, 127, 129 Crown Hall,
Chicago:
Hedrich Blessing.
129 Secondary School,
Hunstanton:
'The Architectural Review'.
129 Gatwick Airport:
'The Architects' Journal'.
131, 132 Climatron, St Louis:
Hedrich Blessing.
133 Drop City, Colorado:
Charlotte Trego.
134, 135 Harumi Apartments,
Tokyo:
Y Futagawa.
137 Town Hall, Rodvre:
RIBA.
136, 137 Vuokseniska
Church, Imatra:
Leonardo Mosso.
138, 139 Highpoint I and II,
Highgate:
Dell and Wainwright/
'The Architectural Review'.
140 Roehampton housing:
H. de Burgh Galwey/
'The Architectural Review'.
141, 142 Park Hill housing,
Sheffield:
Roger Mayne/
'The Architectural Review'.
144, 145 Habitat, Montreal:
'The Architects' Journal'.
146, 147 Town Centre,
Cumbernauld:
'The Architectural Review'.
148, 150 Brasilia, Brazil:
David Crease/
Oscar Niemeyer.
152 Chandigarh:
Courtesy Willy Boesiger.
155 CLASP School, Milan:
COI, London and Publifoto,
Milan.
155 SCSD Prototype school,
Palo Alto:
EFL, New York.
156 Bauhaus Buildings,
Dessau:
Lucia Moholy.
158 Schindler/Chase House,
Los Angeles:
Dan O'Neill.
159 Lovell/Health House,
Los Angeles:
Julius Schulman.
160, 161 Chebel Sootum,
Teheran:
Felix Semuely and Partners
and Frank Newby.
162, 163 Philharmonie,
Berlin:
Professor Dr. Ing Eh
Scharoun.

165, 166, 167 National
Gallery, Berlin:
Mies Van der Rohe/
David L. Hirsch.